Multi Talented Singer

P.B.SRINIVOS

DR RANGANATH NANDYAL

First published in India in 2018

ISBN: 978-93-88333-16-0

Invincible Publishers
G-120, Sushant Lok III, Sector 57, Gurgaon-122002
Registered Address: Opposite Kasturba Ashram,
Radaur, Haryana–135133

Printed at Thomson Press (India) LTD

Author's Contact Information
Phone No: 99861 82781
Email: r.n.nandyal@gmail.com

Dedicated to

My parents & My teachers

and

Millions of admirers of

P.B. Srinivos

AUTHOR WITH LEGENDS

Top Left - With P. Susheela

Top Right - With S. Janaki

Bottom Left - With Bharathi Vishnuvardhan

Bottom Right - With K. Vishwanath

PREFACE

"Music is the medium through which we express our feelings of joy and sorrow, love and patriotism, penitence and praise. Music is the charm of the soul, the instrument that lifts the mind to higher regions, and the gateway into realms of imagination."

- Carl E. Shore, Famous Western Musicologist

"The science of music must be learnt; the art should be presented aesthetically."

- Nedunuri Krishna Murthy, Famous musician

"From my childhood, I am a citizen of the world."

- P.B. Shrinivos.

I interviewed P.B. Srinivos on 5 February, 2013. He was kind enough to allocate the entire day for me. While discussing the prominent figures in Southern Indian film field, I discovered the greatness of the multi-talented singer.

PBS' mind had a comprehensive sweep, embracing ancient and medieval literatures, and modern scientific thought. He was a multi-faceted personality: a polyglot, a bibliophile, a genius, a melodious singer and an incisive writer all rolled into one; his versatility is enviable. He was a humanist to the core and a practising Universalist like Rabindranath Tagore. He touched the lives of millions of his admirers across the regions. This book is not a biography of PBS. With the intention of projecting him at the national and international levels, I have done my research on PBS as a singer and a writer. Having read the available books and articles on the subject of my research and having analyzed the internal as well as external evidence, I have come to the conclusion that PBS was a multi-talented singer whose muses were *sahitya* as well as *sangeeta*. My present work in English is my humble tribute to the multi talented singer.

The writing of this book is a labor of love and veneration which was made lighter and sweeter with the help of a number of persons. Of these, I can only mention the following to whom my grateful thanks are due:

Ms. Bharathi Vishnuvardhan, who readily agreed to write the Foreword to my book; S.P. Balasubramanyam who paid an emotional tribute to PBS; Dr Krishnamani, son-in law of PBS for his substantial contribution towards publishing the book; my cousin K.Anandmohan (alias Aman Hindusthani) for enlightening me on the intricacies of the genre Ghazal in general and PBS'Ghazals in particular; Ms. Vani Jayaram, Ms. Veena Gayatri, Ms. Devi Ramana Murthy and Ms. K. S. Vasantha Lakshmi for offering their garlands of words as their respective tributes; Ms. P. Senthamilselvi and Ms. R. Vijayalakshmi Iyer for clarifying my doubts on PBS and his Tamil songs; Garani S. Radhakrishnan and Murali, a music teacher and Srinath for assisting me about Kannada film field and PBS'Kannada songs; Echuchuri Murali Dhara Rao for his article on Telugu *Chandassu;* my sister K. Vijayalakshmi and Ramesh Panchakarla for their substantial contribution towards PBS' Telugu songs; Shafi, a critic for his help about Malayalam songs; my nephew S. C. Phanindra for his help in procuring some articles; my niece Satya Seshagiri Vasan for providing some photographs; my wife Padma Nandyal without whose consistent encouragement I wouldn't have completed my project; my daughter Neeharika Nandyal for her timely suggestions, and my son, Ved Nandyal, for his love and affection.

I specially thank Invincible Publishers for publishing my book the way I wanted. I profusely thank Aditi, Anjali and Ashish of Invincible Publishers for their skilful contribution.

TRIBUTE
BY S.P. BALASUBRAHMANYAM

Shri P.B. Srinivos was 'AjataShatru'. He had no enemies. He was a polyglot who wrote thousands of poems in 8 languages. His voice was soft and appealing to the heart. Just as Shri Ghantasala's voice contributed to the growth of the careers of N.T. RamaRao and A. Nageswara Rao, Shri PBS' voice contributed to Kannada Kanthirava Shri Rajkumar's career. Even today, Kannadigas have a lot of veneration for Shri PBS. When I sang an Urdu ghazal written by PBS in the presence of the then Pakistani High Commissioner and other Pakistanis, they highly appreciated it. He called me L.G.Balasubramaniam (L.G means Lucky Guy) as I was lucky to sing for M.G. Ramachandran in almost at the beginning of my career. He made me and my sister sing some of the songs written by him in Telugu, Tamil, Kannada, Malayalam and Hindi for Doordarshan. He used to attend the concerts of a number of musicians and generously shower encomiums on them. He was friendly by nature, unassuming and easily accessible to people. He used to have a permanent corner reserved for him in Woodlands Drive in a hotel where he was always seen with a number of books, pens of different colours and people of different hues and shapes. He was fond of delicious food, especially sweets. He was a very good human being full of magnanimity.

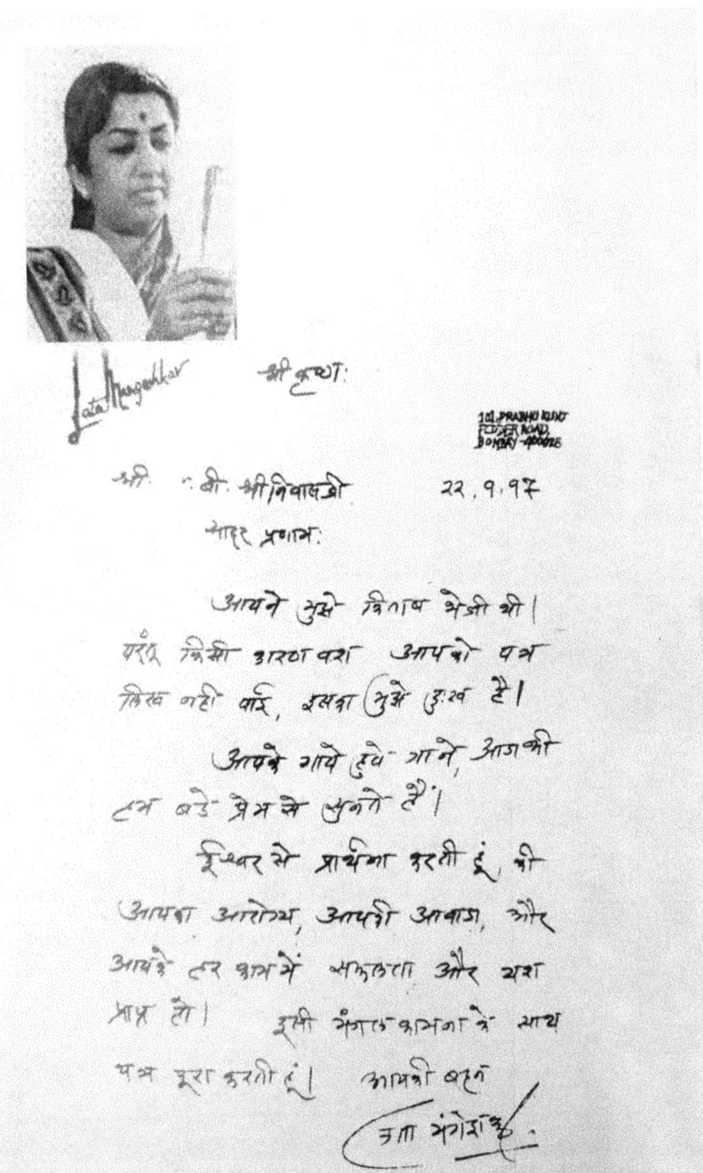

श्री कृष्ण:

101, PRABHU KUNJ
PEDDER ROAD,
BOMBAY-400026

श्री पी. बी. श्रीनिवासजी 22.9.97

सादर प्रणाम:

आपने मुझे किताब भेजी थी।
परंतु किसी कारणवश आपको पत्र
लिख नहीं पाई, इसका मुझे दुःख है।

आपके गाये हुवे गाने, आज भी
हम बड़े प्रेम से सुनते हैं।

ईश्वर से प्रार्थना करती हूं, की
आपका आरोग्य, आपकी आवाज, और
आपके हर काम में सफलता और यश
प्राप्त हो। इसी मंगल कामना के साथ
पत्र पूरा करती हूं। आपकी बहन

लता मंगेशकर.

Letter of Appreciation by Lata Mangeshkar

Manna Dey

Bombay
20th April '97.

My esteemed friend and colleague Shri P. B. Sreenivas has undertaken a unique task of writing a book in eight languages dealing mainly with Fine Arts. Only P.B. could venture to accomplish a near impossible project like 'Pranavam'. I salute him for his undaunted will to achieve excellence in pursuit of Knowledge.

I have always known him to be an ardent student of music but later on he worked very hard for attaining proficiency in the art of writing poems, Geets, Gazals etc. That, indeed, is a great achievement in my estimation.

Lovers of Fine Arts, Good poetry and good music would surely acclaim P.B's work wholeheartedly.

Let us all pray to the Almighty for a resounding success of 'Pranavam'.

Manna Dey

Letter of Appreciation by Manna Dey

J JAYALALITHAA
Chief Minister

SECRETARIAT
Chennai-600 009.

Date 21.9.2005

MESSAGE

Dr. P.B. Sreenivos is indeed a multifaceted genius, poet, musician and singer par excellence. Generations of Indians have basked in the mellifluous magic of his voice, enthralled by the lilting dulcet of his melodious songs which have captured every mood, every emotion that man or woman can feel.

'Pranavam'- a collection of poems in eight languages is yet another marvel from the versatile and fertile mind and pen of Dr. P.B. Sreenivos. In 'Pranavam', we see the nobility of bhakti, beauty, faith, devotion, love, pathos, nature and nationalism flow gently and harmoniously along eight different streams. Reading these poems is, indeed, a uniquely moving experience, which should make every Indian feel proud to be an Indian, despite the diversity of languages. This feeling of oneness and unity in our diversity has been beautifully brought out in his Poem (Number 47) "Pul aur Gul".

I wish Dr. P.B. Sreenivos many more years of a long, healthy and creative life.

J JAYALALITHAA
Chief Minister of Tamil Nadu

Letter of Appreciation by J. Jayalalitha

With Asha Bhonsle and Manna Dey

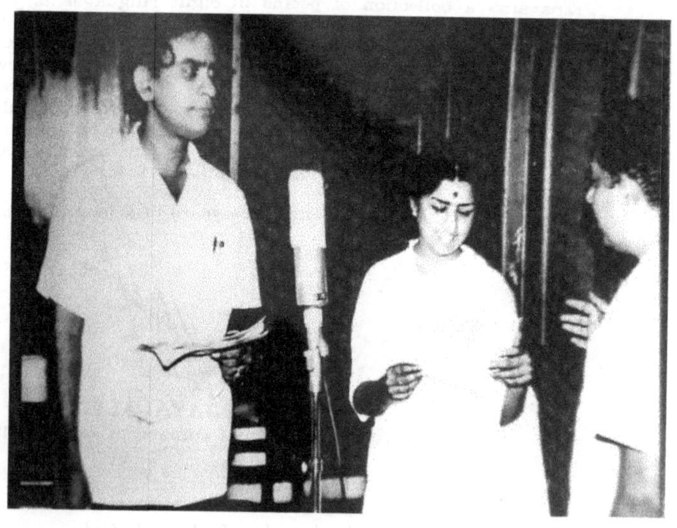

With Lata Mangeshkar

FOREWORD

PADMASHRI BHARATHI VISHNUVARDHAN

Dr. Bharathi Vishnuvardhan

No. 1203, 26th 'A' Main,
35th Cross, 4th 'T' Block,
Jayanagar, Bengaluru-560 041.
Ph. : +91 80 2653 6144
Email : bvardhan001@gmail.com

P.B. Srinivos's singing invokes an image of a decent and noble person. He was a very melodious singer, an excellent writer and above all a magnanimous human being. He was truly humane and affable. He was a cultural icon. Some of his songs were picturized on Dr. Vishnuvardhana, my husband. These songs are my favourite and I listen to them quite often.

As everybody knows the period in which Ghantasala and P.B.S. sang was a platinum period in southern Indian cinema. Both of them were incomparable and had their own spaces.

Prof. Ranganath Nandyal has published a book on Ghantasala in English which had received good reviews. His present book on P.B. Srinivos is also well researched and interestingly written. I am sure it will also receive the same kind of appreciation from people all over. I wish the book a grand success.

Bharathi Vishnu Vardhan

Bharathi Vishnuvardhan
(Padmashree Awardee)

CHAPTER 1

THE BEGINNINGS

"Some are born great

Some achieve greatness

Some have greatness thrust upon them."

-William Shakespeare

"It is not ease but effort, not facility but difficulty that makes man."

-Samuel Smith, Scottish writer and reformer

Prativada Bhayankara Srinivos, famously known as PBS, was born on 22 September, 1930, in Kakinada, Godavari district, combined Madras State. Phanindra Swamy and Seshagiramma were PBS' pious parents. The toddler Srinivos had the sense of tonal quality, volume, and consonance long before he began to sing or knew anything about music. During his growing years, his home resounded with music: his mother, Seshagiramma, played the Veena and sang Carnatic music melodiously. In fact, the child Srinivos learnt music in general and Carnatic music in particular from his mother. PBS' interest in music grew steadily as he listened to the attractive rendering of classical keertanas by his mother.[1] His maternal uncle, Kilambi Krishnamachari, played prominent mythological Telugu plays wherein he sang songs and padyams as well.

PBS, as a young lad, accompanied him to the theatre quite often. Keeping in view the young lad's future career in the cinema field, his maternal uncle gave him the records of Ghantasala who had already become a reckonable singer by then. In perhaps one of the last interviews, he told me that he practiced Ghantasala's padyams from Pushpa Vilapam and Kunti Kumari and the other popular songs of Ghantasala of that period as well. He added that he and his mother would shed tears as they were moved by the pathos that Ghantasala could evoke.[2]

In the later years, Ghantasala became his mentor, his co-singer and his competitor in the Southern Indian cinema field. Ghantasala predicted a bright future for PBS who was just a budding singer then. Fondly recalling his association with the senior singer, PBS told me that Ghantasala used to call him 'Tammudu' (younger brother in Telugu).[3]

Moreover, PBS keenly followed playback singers from the Hindu film field like K.L. Saigal and Pankaj Mullick, Lata Mangeshkar and Shamshad Begum, Mohd.Rafi and Talat Mehmood, Manna Dey and Hemant Kumar.[4]

As a student of Bachelor's in Commerce in P.R. College, Kakinada, he became a popular singer among students and gradually got rid of his initial stage fright.

As a young lad, PBS was intelligent and diligent, receptive and sensitive, imaginative and creative. These innate qualities made him analyse and imbibe the nuances, subtleties and intricacies of playback singing. Being a diligent boy, he practiced the songs sung by the maestros day in and day out to the extent of even neglecting his formal education. His rigorous preparation must have led him to a level of internalization whereby the subtleties and complexities of the technique of playback singing and its aesthetics got embedded in his psyche.

Being aware of the spark in him and being sure of his innate talents, PBS focussed all his energies on becoming a great singer, and decided to dedicate his entire life to music. Even though he never had a formal training in classical music, he learnt Carnatic classical music -like Ekalavya- by listening to the records of well known contemporary classical musicians. He developed such an expertise in classical music that he could encode the ragas of 72 melakartas in a mathematical sutra called the Diamond Key.[5]

"Diligence is the mother of good fortune"

-Benjamin Disraeli[6]

"Music is essentially a play upon feelings with feelings: it is appreciated only so far as it arouses feelings."

-Carl E. Seashore[7]

Young PBS was not only intelligent, but a personification of diligence. His fondness for languages made him imbibe the entire dictionary of English by heart. As a result, he became popular as a 'Mobile Dictionary' in Kakinada circles. He once wrote a sentence in six lines in Sanskrit. He also wrote long winding sentences in English, like Sri Aurobindo, which spread to pages together. With an amazing grasping ability, he repeated the tough Carnatic raga - Todi raga - rendered by the famous Carnatic musician G.V. Balasubramanyam after only listening to him once. His love for languages made him pursue a higher level course in Hindi, namely 'Visharada', from Dakshin Bharat Hindi Prachar Sabha, Madras.[8]

At the behest of his father, PBS joined the Law College in Madras. Nevertheless, the temptation of the tinsel world proved to be irresistible to the young PBS. As his loyalties lay elsewhere, he played a truant in Law College, and went to the studios by skipping his classes.

Meanwhile, worried about his son's future, Phanindraswamy showed PBS' jataka chakram (astrological chart) to an astrologer who predicted that PBS wouldn't come up well in the film field.[9] In spite of the discouraging prediction, with a strong will-power and unflinching faith in his talent, how PBS attained this goal will be analysed on the basis of concrete evidence.

While frequenting Gemini studios, Madras, the budding singer met the founder-producer S.S. Vasan. Emani Shankara Shastri, a family friend of PBS who later became a famous Vainika, was the head of the music department. He conducted the audition for PBS. The budding singer sang the song originally sung by Mohd. Rafi for the movie "Deedar". After listening to the audition song, Emani instantaneously approved it and a person of the stature of S.S. Vasan remarked, "*PBS' humming is enough to melt the stones.*"[10]

The budding singer sang for the first time for a Hindi movie entitled "Mr. Sampath" which was based on a novel written by R.K. Narayan by the same title. PBS sang a few lines individually, and sang in the chorus. Though PBS was from Andhra, his pronunciation of Hindi was impeccable.

The songs 'Aaj Hum Bharat Ki Naari' and 'Chalo Pania Bharan Ko' gave much importance to female voices, but the point to be noted is that he sang in the company of Shamshad Begum, Geeta Roy (who later married the famous thespian Guru Dutt) Talat Mehmood and Jikki. PBS started singing for dubbed movies too.[11]

Providence turned a new leaf in favour of PBS. The movie titled "Jataka Phala" produced by R.Nagendra Rao ironically refuted the prediction of the astrologer and made PBS a reckonable singer. Remakes of the movie "Jataka Phala" were made simultaneously in Telugu and Tamil, their titles being "Jataka Phalam" and "Jadagam". As the directors and music directors of three major film industries in the South listened to the melodies of PBS, offers started falling into PBS' lap for working in different Southern Indian languages.[12]

Notes:

1.Taken from Ranganath Nandyal's 'The Song and its Sweep', The Hindu, 21 June, 2013.

2.Ibid

3.Ibid

4.Taken from P. Senthamilselvi's 'Innisaichakravarti: P. B. Srinivos'

5.Ibid

6.Taken from Carl E. Seashore's 'Psychology of Music'

7.Famous quote by a former Prime Minister of England

8.Taken from P. Senthamilselvi's 'Innisaichakravarti: P.B. Srinivos'

9.Ibid

10.Ibid

11.Taken from a book by Srinath in Kannada "Madhurya Sarvabhowma Dr. P.B. Srinivos - Nadayogiya Sunsadayaana"

12.Ibid

His Parents Phanindra Swamy and Seshagiramma

With his brother Ramanujam

PBS' benefactor Emani Shankara Shastri

CHAPTER 2

KANNADA KASTURI

"*Music is the medium through which we express our feelings of joy and sorrow, love and patriotism, penitence and praise. Music is the charm of the soul, the instrument that lifts mind to higher regions, and the gateway into realms of imagination.*"
-Carl E. Shore, Musicologist[1]

"*The science of music must be learnt; the art should be presented aesthetically.*"

-Nedunuri Krishna Murthy, Musician[2]

With an analogy from Astrophysics, my favourite academic discipline, I will illustrate PBS' growth. In his Kakinada days and the early days of his Madras life, PBS was like a star gazer. Young PBS then felt the power of music just as a star gazer wonders at the stars before he becomes a student of Astrophysics, and then goes on to become a full-fledged astrophysicist. Astrophysics reveals a microcosm of the Universe at large, while to a full-fledged singer, the science of music reveals a microcosm of the structure and operation of the Musical Mind. As the science of music started revealing a microcosm of the hues and colours of the Musical Mind, PBS started evolving as a singer.

With the movie "Jataka Phala", PBS' destiny got awakened. His assiduity to learn and improve his style of singing, his acuity of ear, his quick grasping skill and his phenomenal memory stood him in good stead.

To quote the child prodigy Veena Gayatri who sang 'Dasa Geeta Geeta Sandesham' with PBS, "*His(PBS') melodious voice could execute almost every intricate nuance most effortlessly...I personally liked the soft gentleness of his voice. According to me, the subtle quality of his voice reached out to the deep recesses of the listeners' souls and left a permanent imprint in their hearts.*"[3]

In a similar manner, a critic by the name Shaji makes an insightful comment, "*He(PBS) sang following the North Indian style of light music which placed more emphasis on the little musical details and subtle elaborations than on upfront expressions and emotional heights. He mostly concentrated on the soft feelings underlined by both the music and lyrics.*"[4]

If we analyse the aforementioned comments made by Veena Gayatri and Shaji, we will get to know why PBS emerged as the singer of choice for various melody numbers of great music composers like M.S. Viswanathan, S. Rajeswara Rao, Ghantasala, Ashwatthama, Adi Narayana Rao and K.V. Mahadevan.

With his 'sumadhuram, sushraavyam and sukomalam' voice, he sang his first song for the Kannada thespian Raj Kumar in the movie titled "Ohileshwar" for which music was composed by G.K. Venkatesh. The hero Raj Kumar himself sang a song in the same movie released in 1956. In spite of that, everyone, including Raj Kumar, considered the voice of PBS matching very well with that of the thespian. (It should be noted that the renowned singer Ghantasala sang for Raj Kumar till then.) PBS never looked back after that and sang for Rajkumar for more than two decades. Acknowledging the role played by PBS in the success of his movies, Rajkumar magnanimously remarked, "*Mine is 'Shareera' and PBS is my 'Shaareera'.*"[5]

Just one year before, i.e., in 1955, PBS sang the 'Paapiya jeevana paavanagolisuva' song in the movie "Adarshasati" produced by AVM productions, which established him as a playback singer in Kannada film field. Its music composers were R. Sudarshan and R. Govardhan.

Keen on improving his accent and pronunciation, PBS took the help of R. Nagendra Rao and others. He made an effort to learn and absorb the social and cultural aspects of the

Kannadigas. He also earnestly participated in discussions on the awakening of Kannada language in associations like 'Kannada Prajna'. He assiduously learnt and practiced Purandaradasa Kritis. As a result, the people of Karnataka treated PBS as one of them-even though he was from Andhra and his mother tongue was Telugu.

After attaining perfection in the Kannada language, PBS became cent percent Kannadiga and his records/cassettes/CDs became an inseparable part of Karnataka houses. He stole the hearts of the masses as well as the elite of Karnataka. Soon, PBS attained the status of 'Advitiya Gayaka' in Karnataka, just as Ghantasala was in (combined)Andhra Pradesh and T.M. Sounder Rajan in Tamil Nadu.[6]

Moreover, PBS sang for almost all actors of Southern India, but it is his songs pictured on Dada Saheb Phalke awardee Raj Kumar that would remain forever in the minds of the listeners, especially of Karnataka. The thespian of Karnataka once proclaimed the he was just 'Shareera' (i.e. body in Kannada) while PBS was his 'Shaareera' (i.e. voice in Kannada.)

Number of Kannada songs sung by PBS year wise:

Year-------No. movies released—No. movies with PBS songs

1962---------- 12 movies ------------------------------10

1963-------- 21 movies--------------------------------17

1964-----------18 movies------------------------------16

1965-----------20 movies-------------------------------16

1966-----------20 movies-------------------------------17

1967-----------26 movies-------------------------------23

Moreover, PBS sang for new actors like Uday Kumar, Kalyan Kumar, Rajesh, Sudarshan, Gangadhar, Srinath and Ramgopal. He sang for supporting actors and comedians like Narasimha Raju, Sampath, Eswarappa, Pantulu, Ashwath,

ShivaRam, Ranga Ramesh and Dwarakesh. PBS sang in the new wave movies too. All together, PBS sang in 400-500 Kannada movies.[7]

PBS' Kannada songs can be categorized into four genres: romantic, sad, philosophical, patriotic, devotional and ghazals.

1. Romantic Songs:

i. 'Ravi Varmana Kunchada'

ii. 'Bara Bare Chandada'

ii. 'Naane Veene Neene Thanthi Avane Vainika'

iii. 'Hridaya Veene Viriya taane'

iv. 'Beelli Modada'

v. 'Anuragade Neepaadaleke'

vi. 'Nagu Nagutha Nali Nali

vii. 'Madhura Madhura Vee Manjula Gaana'

2. Sad Songs:

i. 'Baade Hoda Balii inda'

ii. 'Preethine Ana Dyavaru Thande'

3. Philosophical songs:

i. 'Maanava Dehavu Moole Mamsada Tadike'

ii. 'Jaya jaya hey Guru'

iii. 'Amma Amma Nannamma'

4. Patriotic Song

i. 'Apaara keerthi Galisi Meereda Bhavya Naadidu'

ii. 'Kodagina Kaveri'

iii. 'Kannada Naadina Veera Ramaniya'

iv. 'Siri Kannada Nadu'

v. 'Naavaadiva Nudiy Kannada Nudi'

vi. 'Madhyadolage'

5. Devotional songs

i. 'Eesha Ninna Charana Bhajane'

ii. 'Badukidenu Badukidenu'

6. Ghazals: His ghazals are discussed in a separate chapter

Some of the melodious Kannada songs sung by PBS are[8]:

- Naa vaaduva nudiye kannada nudi
- Baare baare chendada cheluvina
- Nagu nagutha nali nali
- Akashave beelali mele
- Ravi varmana kunchad
- Yelli mareyadhe vittala
- Endhendu ninnanu Marethu
- Ilidhu baa thaayi ilidhu baa
- Aadisi nodu beelisi nodu
- Ninadhe nenapu dinavu manadalli
- Binkada singari
- Haadondha haaduvelf
- 'Akashadha Lokadhi Dhoora' from Bettadha Huli
- 'Aadiuthiruva Modagale' from Bettadha Huli
- 'Dhoni Saagali' from Miss Leelavathi
- 'Baara Chandrama' from Swarna Gowri
- 'Baare Nee Cheluve' from Swarna Gowri
- 'Apara Keerthi Galisi' from Vijayanagaradha Veeraputra
- 'Gopura Kandu' from Arishina Kumkuma
- Bande Nee Bande' from Gandondu Hennaru
- 'Aha Idhenu Nade' from Dhoomaketu
- Deena Naa Bandiruve' from Sandhyaa Raaga
- 'Baredhe Neenu Nanna Hesara' from Seetha
- 'Baagilanu Teredu' from Kanakadasa
- 'Olumeya Huve' from Punarjanma
- Anuragadhi Nee Paadaleke

- Dhina Dhina Olumeyu Kandaaga
- Jo Jo Laali naa haduve
- Prema Preethi nanara
- Naa haadalu naa padulu
- Nena bittu reladivelu
- Nasike Inneke
- Kumkuma Haniyet
- Sutta Mutta yaru illa
- Gauri Manohari
- Magiye cheruvall
- Havina Hanunade
- Bela divya lagibu
- Devaragudi
- Swara tande saubhagya8

Why did PBS' chances as a playback singer dim in the late 1970's?

The reasons are ut infra:

A. From 1956 to 1974, PBS was the voice of the famous thespian Raj Kumar in Kannada film field. However, when PBS was not available for singing for the movie"Sampattige Sawaal", music composer G.K. Venkatesh encouraged the hero Raj Kumar to sing the song 'Yaare Koogadali' himself, which was supposed to be sung by PBS. With that song, Raj Kumar started his singing career again which had stopped after the movie "Ohileswara". Thus began his journey as the most famous actor-singer that the Southern Indian film industry has ever seen. Unfortunately, it synchronised with the downfall of the melodious singer PBS (i.e., the real playback singer). Later, in Raj Kumar's movies, PBS was given a song to sing, but the decline led to his disappearance from the Kannada movie world. Even though he occasionally sang a song or two, the market for PBS was over.

B. By mid-70's, important changes started taking place in all aspects of film making in Tamil. Till then, for Shivaji Ganesan and MGR, most songs were sung by T.M. Sounderajan and for Gemini Ganesan, PBS sang melodious songs. However, since time and tide wait for none, the senior actors like Shivaji and MGR were ageing, and were yielding their place to young actors like Kamal Haassan. As a result, senior singers like TMS and PBS found it difficult to lend their voices to the younger stars. It synchronized with the advent of the new wave music composer, Illaiyaraja. With his penchant for western and folk tunes, Illaiyaraja used to prefer Dasettan for classical songs and S.P. Balu for light classical tunes. In the process, PBS got sidelined.[9]

C. When S.P. Balasubrahmanyam (S.P. Balu) entered the Southern Indian film field in the mid 1960's, he was just 20 years old-about 20 years younger than PBS. With his youthful vigour, marketing skills, admirable grasping abilities and excellent mimicry skills, SPB's star rose quickly and steadily on the firmament of the Southern Indian Cinema. With his deft mimicry skills, he could sing for old actors like MGR and Shivaji, and young actors like Kamal Haassan and Rajanikanth.

D. The situation is similar, if not identical, in the Telugu movie field. The reigning king Ghantasala suddenly passed away in 1974, which synchronized with the emergence of the young and energetic S.P. Balu. Consequently, PBS was sidelined.

E. PBS was popular in Malayalam film field too, but the young classically trained Malayalee singer K.J. Yesudas was preferred by music composers.

F. It is a well-known fact that PBS was a thorough gentleman. His genial nature, an innate aversion for campaigning for himself or projecting himself in the days of cut-throat competition with the youngsters was also responsible for the fading of his popularity.

Notes:

1. Taken from Carl E. Seashore's'Psychology of Music'. Dover Publications Inc., New York.

2. Taken from 'Mee Ghantasala', P.117

3. Taken from Veena Gayatri, email letter to the author

4. Taken from Shaji's article on PBS, "P.B. Srinivas: From the Springtime of Film Music"

5. Taken from Srinath's book "Madhurya Sarvabhowma Dr. P.B. Srinivos" on PBS in Kannada

6. Ibid

7. Ibid

8. Ibid

9.Taken from my interview with Bharathi Vishnuvardhan and Suggestions from S.C. Phanindra

With P. Susheela

With S. Janaki

CHAPTER 3

THITHIKKUM (SWEET) TAMIL

"*There is a tide in the affairs of men, which taken at the flood, leads on to fortu*ne."

-William Shakespeare

"*When melody was given higher importance, I entered the field. It was my luck.*"

-P.B. Srinivos[1]

After successfully singing two songs each in the trilingual movie released as Jataka Phala(Kannada), Jataka Phalam(Telugu) and Jadagam(Tamil), PBS got an opportunity to sing the song 'Anbodu Inbamaga' in the movie "Viduthalai". This song had a mark of the unique style and rendering of PBS.It should be noted that he sang two songs for the movie "Jadagam", which are 'Sindhanai en Selvame' and 'Mooda Nambikkai'.[2]

In 1957, the professional career of PBS took a big leap with a duet with Jikki 'Gamagamavena' in the movie "Samaya Sanjeevi". 'Ondru semda anbu maruma' for the film "Makkalai Petra Magara Asi" and the song 'Kannukku nere minnidum taarai' from the film "Magdalanattu Mary" were released in the same year. In 1959, he sang the song 'Ingum pongum vennila veesuthe' for Gemini Ganesan in the movie "Veerapandya Kattabomman". The credit for making PBS sing for Gemini Ganesan the first time goes to G. Ramanathan. The multi-talented singer sang for Kaadhai Mannan for 16 years in various genres: romantic, sad, philosophical and devotional.

For the film "Adbutha Veettu Penn", AdiNarayana Rao of the movie "Suvarna Sundari" fame, made PBS sing three enthralling songs for the movie “Vaadaatha Pushpamay”. The songs are:

i. ‘VanitmManiye’

ii. ‘Kannaale pesi pesi’

iii. ‘Maalarayil malarcholaiyil’

However, PBS’ popularity touched a new high with the song he sang for the movie “Paavamannippu” which was pictured on Gemini Ganesan. The ever-green song is ‘Kalangaliil aval vasantham’ composed by the admirable composer duo M.S. Viswanathan-Ramamurthy. Thus started PBS’ songs for the popular Kaadhai Mannan.[3]

Look at the comments made by no less a composer than M.S. Viswanathan - “*In those days many believed that the voice of TMS suited Sivaji and MGR, and that A.M. Rajah was only the voice of Gemini Ganesan. I wanted to change this. I got PBS to sing for Gemini Ganesan. Though he had already sung for me and other composers, that was the first time he sang for a big hero. Later he also sang for Shivaji and MGR.*”[4]

PBS’ Tamil songs can be categorized under 5 genres: romantic, sad, philosophical, patriotic, devotional and ghazals:

1. Romantic songs:

i. ‘Pon en ben’ from “Police Kaaran Magan”

ii. ‘Poga Poga Theriyum’ from “Server Sundaram”

iii. ‘Parthen Sirithen’ from “Veerabhimanyu”

iv. ‘Thennan Keetru Oonjalile’ from “Paathai Teriyuthu parr”

v. ‘Paal Vannam Paruvam Kandu’ from “Paasam”

vi. ‘Poojaikku Vandha Malare Va’ from “Paadha Kaanikkai”

2. Sad Songs:

i.’Nilave Ennidam Nirungathe’ from “Ramu”

ii.'Kangale Kangale' from "Vazhkkaipaadagu"

iii.'Endha Oor Entdravane' from "Katturoja"

3. Philosophical Songs:

i. 'Udalukku Uyir Kaaval' from "Manappandhal"

ii. 'Mayakkama Kalakkama' from "Sumaithangi"

iii. 'Manidhan Enbavan' from "Sumaithangi"

iv. 'Edho Manidhan' from "Panithirai"

4. Devotional Songs:

i. 'Paada Paada Thein' from "Bhakta Sabari"

ii. 'Avanallal Puvi Mele' from "Prema Pasam"

iii. 'Anbu Vadivaga Nindrai' from "Swami Ayyappan"

iv. 'Anaithaalum Neeye Adithaalum Neeye' from "Prema Pasam"

Some of the Sonorous Tamil songs sung by PBS are:

- Kaalangalil aval vasantham — from Paavamannippu
- Nilave ennidam nerungadhe — from Ramu
- Maadi malae maadi Patti neramillai — from Kaadhalikka
- Mouname paarvaiyail — from Kodimalar
- Nilavukku enmel ennadi kobam — from Policekaran Magal
- Roja malare Raja Kumari — from Veerathirumagan
- Paal vannam Paruvam kandu — from Paasam
- Paadatha pattellam padavandhel — from Veerathirumagan
- Ninaippadellam Nadanthu vittaal — from Nenjil oru alayam
- Mayakkama Kalakkama — from Sumaithangi
- Manidan Enbavan Daivamaaagalaam — from Sumaithangi
- Netru varai nee yaaro — from Vazhkai padagu
- Udalukku uyir kaval — from Manappandhai
- Indha mandrathil oadivarum — from Policekaran Magal
- Anubhavam pudumai neramillai — from kaadhalikka
- Avalparandhu ponaale — from Paar magalai paar

13	Kaatruveliyidai kannamma	Mohana Kalyani	Kappal Otiye Tamiazhn
14		Mohanam	KPT
15	Podhigai Malai Uchiyile	Natabhairavi	Thiruviaiyadal
16	Malayail Malar	Hamsadhwani	Adutha Veettuppenn
17	Kaaniyo Paaho Karaando	Pahaadi	Kaatru Veliyidai
18	Adiparashakti	Raagamalika	Aadiparashakti

Notes

1. Taken from P. Senthamilselvi's 'Innisai Chakravarthi P.B. Srinivos'

2. Taken from Shaji's article on PBS "P.B. Srinivas: From the Springtime of Film Music"

3. Ibid

4. Taken from Ranganath Nandyal 'The Song and its Sweep'. The Hindu, 21 June, 2003

8, Nungambakkam High Road,
Madras 600 034, S. India
Phone: 82 79530 82 57 667

Date ....

P.B.S என்ற மூன்றெழுத்தை
இந்தியாவில் அறியாதவர்கள் இல்லை
அவர் ஒரு Play Back Singer
என்பது அவர் initials இலேயே இருக்கிறது.

[illegible]

Appreciation Letter by Gemini Ganeshan

Gemini Ganesh
Film Artiste, Producer, Director

8, Nungambakkam High Road,
Madras 600 034. S. India.
Phone: 82-79630 82 67 687

Date.............................

[illegible] P.B.S [illegible]

[illegible]

[illegible] P.B.S [illegible]

[illegible]

[illegible]

With Gemini Ganeshan

With M.G.Ramachandran& Shivaji Ganeshan

CHAPTER 4
SUNDARA TELUGU

"*Music is a piece of art, which creates an aural world of emotions.*"

-T.M. Krishna, Musician and Musicologist[1]

We have analysed how the movie "Jataka Phala" in Kannada released in 1953 and its retakes, "Jadagam" in Tamil and "Jataka Phalam" in Telugu led to the awakening of PBS' destiny in his professional career. The song 'Ela Digulela Kalamu Maarunule MaruvakeBela Digulela' was from the movie "Jataka Phalam".

In 1956, P.B. Srinivos sang his first hit song in Telugu, 'Bhayamela o manasa' for the movie "Bhale Ramudu". Its famous music composer, S. Rajeswara Rao, justified his choice ut infra:

"*Many asked me why I had brought in P.B. Srinivos when Ghantasala was already there. I like the deep voice of P.B. Srinivos with its soft movements. I thought it would be something novel and a great change from Ghantasala.*"[2]

In 1960, the highly talented music composer S. Rajeswara Rao recognized the talents of PBS and made him sing for N.T. Ramarao in the movie "Rani Ratnaprabha". The song is 'Anuragamu olike'.

In a similar manner, renowned music composer M.S. Viswanathan, who made PBS sing for Gemini Ganesan in Tamil, declared, "I also made him (PBS) sing for N.T. Rama Rao in Telugu. Many opposed my move saying that only the voice of Ghantasala suited N.T. Rama Rao. But I resolutely went on to make PBS sing for N.T. Rama Rao. The song 'Bujji Bujji Paapaayi' was widely appreciated and became very famous."[3]

PBS' Telugu songs can be categorized into seven genres: romantic, sad, philosophical, devotional, padyams, strotras and ghazals:

1. Romantic Songs:

i. 'Adi Oka Idile Atanike Tagule'—"Preminchi Chudu"

ii. 'Vennela Reyi Entho Chali'—"Preminchi Chudu"

iii. 'Andaala O Chiluka' —"Letha Manasulu"

iv. 'Neeli Kannula Needalalona'—"Gudi Gantalu"

v. 'Ninne Ninne Neeve Neeve'—"Intiki Deepam Illale"

2. Sad Songs:

i. 'Chigurakula ooyalalo'—"Kanistable Kooturu"

ii. 'Maguvala valalo'—"Pelli Roju"

3. Philosophical Songs:

i. 'Talachinade Jariginada'—"Aada Bratuku"

ii. 'Bujji Bujji Papaayi'—"Aada Bratuku"

iii. 'Evariki Evaru Kaapala'—"Preminchi Chudu"

4. Devotional Songs:

i. 'Sri Ramachandraha Aasrita'—"Shanti Nivasam"

ii. 'Emi Rama Katha'—"Bhakta Sabari"

iii. 'Ranaiunnadu Srihari'—"Bhakta Sabari"

iv. 'Sarvamangala Nama Rama'—"Bhakta Potana"

5. Padyams:

I 'Chesina Karmaye Jeeviki Chukkani'—"Bhishma"

ii. 'Katuka kanti neeru Chanu kattu'—"Bhakta Potana"

iii. 'Ala Vaikuntha Purammulo'—"Bhakta Potana"

6. Stotrams:

i. 'Sriman Mahamangala'—"Bhakta Potana"

Other Storams are given in a separate section

7. Ghazals:

PBS' Telugu Ghazals are given in a separate chapter

PBS sang 652 songs in 317 Telugu movies. Some of PBS' enthralling Telugu songs are[4]:

S.NO	YEAR	FILM NAME	SONG
1	1954	JATAKA PHALAM	YELAA DIGULELAA EE KAALAM
2	1956	BHALE RAMUDU	BANGARU BOMMA
3	1956	BHALE RAMUDU	BHAYAMELA O MANASA
4	1956	BHALE RAMUDU	GOPALA DEVA
5	1956	BHALE RAMUDU	PREMA KRITIVO
6	1956	NAGULA CHAVITHI	SAAGARA MEEDUTA
7	1956	NAGULA CHAVITHI	SURAMYA SEELA
8	1956	NAGULA CHAVITHI	VANDE SHAMBHUMUMAA PATIM

9	1956	PENKI PELLAM	LEDOYI LEDOYI VERE HAAYI
10	1957	ALLAVUDDIN ADBHUTA DEEPAM	SOGASARI DAANANAYA
11	1957	BHALE AMMAAYILU	CHEETIKI MAATIKI
12	1957	BHALE AMMAAYILU	NAANYAMAINA SARUKUNDI
13	1957	DAAMPATYAM	ATI SWEETUGA BALU NEETUGAA
14	1957	DAAMPATYAM	EENAATI AMMAAYILU BABO
15	1957	KUTUMBA GOWRAVAM	AANANDAALE
16	1957	RANI RANGAMMA(D)	KALALU TARIMCHU
17	1957	RANI RANGAMMA(D)	MANAPAI SAPINCHE DAIVAM
18	1957	RANI RANGAMMA(D)	ORACHOOPU KANNAMTA
19	1957	SWAYAM PRABHA	AANANDA MADHURA
20	1957	TOWN BUS(D)	LADY LADY
21	1957	VADDANTE PELLI	YE NOTA VINNA

22	1957	VEGU CHUKKA(D)	MUNUSAAGI PODAME
23	1957	VEGU CHUKKA(D)	TEMPUNNADI TELIVUNNADI
24	1958	ANNA TAMMUDU	CHINNARI CHETULA
25	1958	ATTA OKINTI KODALE	PAILA PAILA
26	1958	ATTA OKINTI KODALE	RAMMANTE VACHHARU
27	1958	CHENCHU LAKSHMI	AKHILA(PADYAM)
28	1958	CHENCHU LAKSHMI	CHILAKA GORINKA
29	1958	DONGALUNNARU JAGRATTA	VALAPE PULAKINTA
30	1958	INTI GUTTU	CHITAARU KOMMA MEEDA
31	1958	KARTAVARAAYANI KATHA	AANANDA MOHANA
32	1958	KARTAVARAAYANI KATHA	KAAVAALI KAAVAALI
33	1958	KARTAVARAAYANI KATHA	MOOGE CHEEKATI
34	1958	KARTAVARAAYANI KATHA	OKKASAARI CHOODAVA
35	1958	KONDAVEETI DONGA(D)	OKKARIKE IDDARAYA

36	1958	KONDAVEETI DONGA(D)	TAMALA PAAKU
37	1958	SRI KRISHNA GARADI	BHALIRE(PADYAM)
38	1958	SRI KRISHNA GARADI	ENTA GHANUDAVAYYA
39	1958	SRI KRISHNA GARADI	PANDUGALU
40	1958	SRI RAMA BKHAKTA HANUMAN(D)	LEMMOYI
41	1958	SRI RAMANJANEYA YUDDHAM	AAKU LALAMULU TINUCHU
42	1958	SRI RAMANJANEYA YUDDHAM	DHARMAMU DHARMAMANCHITU
43	1958	SRI RAMANJANEYA YUDDHAM	KSHEMAMBE KADAA
44	1958	SRI RAMANJANEYA YUDDHAM	NEE PRADHAANAMBU
45	1958	SRI RAMANJANEYA YUDDHAM	NENE SRI RAGHUVAMSH
46	1958	SRI RAMANJANEYA YUDDHAM	OKATE MAATAYATANNA(PADYAM)
47	1958	VIJAYA KOTA VEERUDU(D)	HARA HAROM TIRIGI
48	1958	VIJAYA KOTA VEERUDU(D)	HE HE HE RAAJA

49	1959	CHEVILO RAHASYAM(D)	CHELAREGI UOOGI SAAGENE
50	1959	DAIVA BALAM	ANDAALA O CHANDAMAAMA
51	1959	DAIVA BALAM	CHIRU CHIRU NAVVULA PUVVULA
52	1959	DAIVA BALAM	NINNU VARINCHE
53	1959	HANUMAN PATALA VIJAYAM(D)	SODHINCHAKU LEDA
54	1959	JAYA VIJAYA	GILIGINTALA CHAKKILIGINTAL AO
55	1959	JAYA BHERI	MADI SARADA DEVI
56	1959	JIMBO(D)	EE JAGAMIDI KALA KAADU
57	1959	JIMBO(D)	EE MAYA JAGATIN
58	1959	KUTURU KAPURAM	ALUGUTAYE YERUNGANI(PAD YAM)
59	1959	KUTURU KAPURAM	LADDU LADDU TAAJA LADDU
60	1959	KUTURU KAPURAM	NE ROOPAKAIGADE(P ADYAM)
61	1959	MAA INTI MAHA LAKSHMI	AAMANI MADHU YAAMINI

62	1959	MAHISHASURA MARDANI(D)	MAANIKYA VEENAAM
63	1959	MAHISHASURA MARDANI(D)	SREEHARI MURAARI
64	1959	MANORAMA	OHOHO KANTAMMA
65	1959	PEDDA KODALU(D)	AMRUTA YOGAM VACCHE
66	1959	PEDDA KODALU(D)	DINGIRI DINGIRI MEENAAKSHI
67	1959	PELLI MEEDA PELLI	ANDI ANDAKAPOYA
68	1959	PELLI MEEDA PELLI	CHIRUNAVVULA
69	1959	PELLI MEEDA PELLI	CHIRUNAVVULA NAVA VASANTAM
70	1959	PELLI MEEDA PELLI	KANULANU
71	1959	RAJA MALAYA SIMHA	AASE VIRISE NAVA JEEVANAME
72	1959	RAJA MALAYA SIMHA	SANTOSHAMULA YANDU
73	1959	SAMPOORNA RAMAYANAM(D)	PAADUKALE
74	1959	VEERA BHASAKARUDU	ELAAGE SUKHAALA
75	1959	VEERA GHATOTKACHA(D)	BHALASAALIVI LE IKACHAALU

76	1959	VEERA GHATOTKACHA(D)	THOTALONI GULAABI
77	1959	VEERAPANDYA KATTA BRAHMANA(D)	IMPU SOMPU
78	1960	ANNA CHELLELU	BANDI NADIPINCHA BRATUKU
79	1960	ANNA CHELLELU	GANGIREDLA GANGANNA
80	1960	ANNA CHELLELU	PANTA NEETI GUNTA KAADA
81	1960	ANNA CHELLELU	TEEGAMALLI POOSENURAA
82	1960	ANNAPOORNA	MANASEMITO
83	1960	BAGADAD GAJADONGA(D)	NAAKE DUMKEE KOTTEV
84	1960	BAGADAD GAJADONGA(D)	VAALU CHOOPULA MANASULU
85	1960	BHAKTA SABHARI	EMI RAAMA KATHA
86	1960	BHAKTA SABHARI	MAARAALI MAARAALI MANA TEERULU
87	1960	BHAKTA SABHARI	RAAMAA NYAAYAMAA
88	1960	BHAKTA SABHARI	RAANAI YUNNAADU SREEHARI

89	1960	BHAKTA VIJAYAM(D)	JAGAMANTAA BHRAAMTIYE
90	1960	BHAKTA VIJAYAM(D)	JAGATI NE NELAVE
91	1960	BHAKTA VIJAYAM(D)	JAYA PANDURANGA HARI
92	1960	BHAKTA VIJAYAM(D)	OMKAARA SARASIYANDU
93	1960	BHAKTA VIJAYAM(D)	SARVA SAAKSHIYU NEEVE
94	1960	CHIVARAKU MIGILEDI	AAKAASAANA HAMSALAGAA
95	1960	DEVANTAKUDU	ENTA MADHURA SEEMA
96	1960	DEVANTAKUDU	GO GO GONGURA
97	1960	DEVANTAKUDU	HO DHIMI DHIMI DHIMI
98	1960	DEVANTAKUDU	JAGAMANTHA MARINADI
99	1960	DEVANTAKUDU	O NAADU TANDRI
100	1960	DEVANTAKUDU	USHA PARINAYAM
101	1960	JAGANNAATAKAM	NANNU CHEKONI NAAVAA

102	1960	JAGANNAATAKAM	OM NAMAH PARAMAARDHE
103	1960	JALSA RAYUDU	ANDAALA SEEMALO
104	1960	JIMBO NAGARA PRAVESAM(D)	GANTI PADE NAA HRUDAYAM
105	1960	JIMBO NAGARA PRAVESAM(D)	KALLATONE PAADI
106	1960	KADEDDULU EKARAM NELA	CHALULE
107	1960	KANAKADURGA POOJA MAHIMA	ANURAAGA SEEMA
108	1960	KANAKADURGA POOJA MAHIMA	JAYA JAYA NAMO KANAKADURGA
109	1960	KANAKADURGA POOJA MAHIMA	OM KAARA PAMJARA
110	1960	KROTTA DAARI(D)	NEEVAADITE EVARAADARU
111	1960	KROTTA DAARI(D)	VINTAINA LOKAMAYYAA
112	1960	MAGAVAARI MAAYALU	MADILONA YEMO
113	1960	MAGAVAARI MAAYALU	YE KSHANAMU
114	1960	MAHARATHI KARNA(D)	MANASAA ANTAA MAAYELE
115	1960	MAHARATHI KARNA(D)	NANNU BANDHINCHU(PADYAM)

116	1960	MAMAKU TAGGA ALLUDU	NEETAINA AMMAAYI
117	1960	MUGGURU VEERULU	CHALUNAYAA IKA CHALUNAYAA
118	1960	MUGGURU VEERULU	IDDARINI KATTUKUNTE
119	1960	NAGA MOHINI(D)	O MANUSHYA LOKAIKA
120	1960	NITYA KALYANAM PACCHA TORANAM	AASALU NEEVU
121	1960	NITYA KALYANAM PACCHA TORANAM	EVARIKI VAARE
122	1960	NITYA KALYANAM PACCHA TORANAM	NEE MADI
123	1960	PATIVRATA(D)	CHINNAARI VANNELAADI
124	1960	PATIVRATA(D)	SA SA PADAMMAA MOHANAA
125	1960	PILLALU TECCHINA CHALLANI RAJYAM	CHITTI CHEEMALU(PADY AM)
126	1960	PILLALU TECCHINA CHALLANI RAJYAM	JAATAKA BALAME BALAMAYYAA
127	1960	PILLALU TECCHINA CHALLANI RAJYAM	NINNU CHOOCHI
128	1960	RAMA SUNDARI	ANDAALA BAALA

129	1960	RAMA SUNDARI	NEELI MEGHAALALO(PA DYAM)
130	1960	RANI RATNA PRABHA	ANURAAGAMU VELASE EE REYI
131	1960	RANI RATNA PRABHA	EKKADA DACHAVO SIPAAYI
132	1960	RENUKADEVI MAHATYAM	DEVUNI MAAYA
133	1960	RENUKADEVI MAHATYAM	HARA HARA SIVA SIVA
134	1960	RENUKADEVI MAHATYAM	JANANI JANANI PARAMESHUNI
135	1960	RENUKADEVI MAHATYAM	SADGUNA NIKURUMBA
136	1960	RUNANU BANDHAM	ANDAMAINA BAAVAA
137	1960	RUNANU BANDHAM	EHE EHE NEELU TODAALI
138	1960	RUNANU BANDHAM	OHO OYYAARI JAHIRI
139	1960	RUNANU BANDHAM	RAAVELA ANDAALA
140	1960	SAHASRA SIRCCHEDA APOORVA CHINTAMANI	ANURAAGAMULO MANA

141	1960	SAHASRA SIRCCHEDA APOORVA CHINTAMANI	GOOTILONA CHILUKA
142	1960	SAMAAJAM	CHAKKANI CHUKKA
143	1960	SAMAAJAM	KANAPADAKUNT E NEMO
144	1960	SAMAAJAM	KANULA NIDURA RAAKAPOTE
145	1960	SAMAAJAM	SAMAAJA MIDIYENAA
146	1960	SANCHAARI(D)	NAATYA VILOLA AADEVELA
147	1960	SANCHAARI(D)	PUVVULU CHINDE TENIYALANDI
148	1960	SANCHAARI(D)	SANGEETA DEVATA
149	1960	SANTI NIVAASAM	SREE RAGHURAAM
150	1960	SRIKRISHNA RAYABARAM	EVARIKI VAARE INKA
151	1960	SRIKRISHNA RAYABARAM	RAAVAYYA NANDA KISORA
152	1960	SRIKRISHNA RAYABARAM	VAASAVI TODA(PADYAM)
153	1961	AMULYA KANUKA(D)	MAHESWARI TRIBUVANA

154	1961	ANUMANAM(D)	JABILLI KANNAANU
155	1961	ARABBI VEERUDU JABAK(D)	MADILONA REGE
156	1961	BAVA MARADALLU	GANGAMMA TALLI
157	1961	BHAKTA JAYADEVA	RADHA MANORAMANA
158	1961	CHINNANNA SAPATHAM(D)	TAMBI TAMBI
159	1961	EVARU DONGA(D)	VALAPINCHE
160	1961	EVARU DONGA(D)	CHIRU NAGAVE
161	1961	EVARU DONGA(D)	PADUNAARU KALALENU
162	1961	GULLO PELLI	TRULLIPADI TOLIVALAPU
163	1961	GULLO PELLI	CHINTALANDUNA CHITIKIPOYINA
164	1961	IDDARU MITRULU	CHAKKANI CHUKKA
165	1961	INDRAJIT	AADAVE VAYAARI
166	1961	INDRAJIT	NAMO NAMO NARAYANA
167	1961	INTIKI DEEPAM ILLAALE	NEEVE NEEVE NINNE NINNE

168	1961	INTIKI DEEPAM ILLAALE	YEVARIKI YEVARU KAAPALAA
169	1961	JEBU DONGA(D)	CHAKKANI CHIRUNAGAVE
170	1961	JEBU DONGA(D)	HAAYIGAA NATYAMANDUTA M
171	1961	KANNA KODUKU	CHAATUKU POYE JAABILLI
172	1961	KANNA KODUKU	EE REYI HAAYI EE POOLA TAAVI
173	1961	KANNA KODUKU	MADILO ENNO BAADHALUNNA
174	1961	KANNA KODUKU	NAA MADILONI KORIKALU
175	1961	KANNA KODUKU	PUVVULU PAAPALU DEVUNI
176	1961	KANYAKA PARAMESWARI MAHATYAM(D)	JEEVITAMU DHANYAME
177	1961	KORADA VEERUDU(D)	NEEVU NENU ILALO EVARO
178	1961	KRISHNA PREMA	NAADU TULAABHAARA(P ADYAM)
179	1961	KRISHNA PREMA	SARVA SARVAMSHA
180	1961	KRISHNA PREMA	SUDHAA MADHURAMU

181	1961	MADANA MANJARI(D)	CHELI CHAMELI RANGA
182	1961	MAYA MACHINDRA(D)	GHAL GHAL MOHINI
183	1961	PAPA PARIHARAM(D)	KANNA TALLINI KANULAARA
184	1961	PAPA PARIHARAM(D)	LOKANIKE NAVA
185	1961	PAPA PARIHARAM(D)	VISWA SEEMALO
186	1961	PAAPAALA BHAIRAVUDU(D)	KAVITAYU NEEVENA
187	1961	PENDLI PILUPU	TELUSUKO O JAVARALA
188	1961	RANI CHENNAMMA(D)	ANURAAGAALE PAADENU
189	1961	RANI CHENNAMMA(D)	DEVU DEVU DEVUDANA
190	1961	RANI CHENNAMMA(D)	KSHEMASAAGAR A LOKAPAALAN
191	1961	RANI CHENNAMMA(D)	MAHARAJA YOGAMITU
192	1961	RANI CHENNAMMA(D)	MAATRUDEVATA NU KAANAGA
193	1961	SAMPOORNA RAMAYANAM(D)	OHO SRI RAMA
194	1961	SHANTA	KALALONI KAVITA LATA

195	1961	SHANTA	PALU VANNELA PAVURAMA
196	1961	SITA(LAV-KUSA)-(D)	PAAVANA MOORTHY GAADHANE
197	1961	SITA(LAV-KUSA)-(D)	PAAVANA MOORTHY SEETAA MAATA
198	1961	SITARAMA KALYANAM	BHOOMIKI(PADYAM)
199	1961	SITARAMA KALYANAM	CHIRUNAGAVU(PADYAM)
200	1961	SITARAMA KALYANAM	DEVA DEVA
201	1961	SITARAMA KALYANAM	INUPA KAATTADAAL(PADYAM)
202	1961	SITARAMA KALYANAM	NANDINI(PADYAM)
203	1961	TANDRULU KODUKULU	KUPPALA KAAVALI(PADYAM)
204	1961	TANDRULU KODUKULU	OHOHO SUNDARI NEE ANDAMENA
205	1961	TANDRULU KODUKULU	UNNA MAATA
206	1961	USHA PARINAYAM	ADIGO MANA PREMA
207	1961	USHA PARINAYAM	BRATIKI PHALAMBEMI

208	1961	VARALAKSHMI VRATAM	ANDAALU
209	1961	VARALAKSHMI VRATAM	JAYA JAGADEESHA(TITLE SONG)
210	1961	VIPLAVA VEERUDU(D)	KALALA RANI KANIPINCHE
211	1961	VIPLAVA VEERUDU(D)	RAAGAME RAAGAME ANURAAGAME
212	1961	VIRISINA VENNELA(D)	OHO OHO BABY RAAVELAA
213	1961	VIRISINA VENNELA(D)	PAARIPODUVAA PENIKI PILLAVA
214	1962	AADAESA VEERULU(D)	RAA CHILUKA KANAVELA
215	1962	APPAGINTALU	MALLE PANDIRI
216	1962	ATMA BANDHUVU	DAKKENULE
217	1962	BEESHMA	BAAVA KARNUDE
218	1962	BEESHMA	CHESINA KARMAYE(PADYAM)
219	1962	BEESHMA	MANASULONI KORIKA
220	1962	BEESHMA	NANNU NEVVAANIGAA(PADYAM)

221	1962	BEESHMA	PAANDAVULANU(PADYAM)
222	1962	BEESHMA	PORU NASTAMBU(PADY AM)
223	1962	BEESHMA	SAMARA MATANCHU(PADY AM)
224	1962	DAKSHA YAGNAM	IDI CHAKKANI LOKAMU
225	1962	DAKSHA YAGNAM	JAABILI
226	1962	DASAVATARAMULU(D)	YADAA YADAAHI(SLOKA M)
227	1962	GAALI MEDALU	NAVA RAGAALU
228	1962	IDDARU KODUKULU(D)	PAATA OKA PAATA
229	1962	IDDARU KODUKULU(D)	PATTU CHEERA
230	1962	KHAIDI KANNAIAH	EE NIJAM TELUSUKO
231	1962	KHADGA VEERUDU(D)	KANNERE MUNNEERAI
232	1962	KULAGOTRALU	MAMA KAARU MABBULA
233	1962	KULAGOTRALU	RAAVE RAAVE BAALA

234	1962	MADANA MKAMARAJU KATHA	NAA KOTI SWAPNAALU(PAD YAM)
235	1962	MADANA MKAMARAJU KATHA	NEELI MEGHA MAALAVO(1)
236	1962	MADANA MKAMARAJU KATHA	NEELI MEGHA MAALAVO(2)
237	1962	MADANA MKAMARAJU KATHA	TELIPODAAMU
238	1962	NAGARJUNA	KAASI VISWESWARUN(P ADYAM)
239	1962	NUVVAA NENAA	VUYYAALALOOG E NAA MADI
240	1962	NUVVAA NENAA	KORADAA PATTINA MAA RAAJA
241	1962	NUVVAA NENAA	MELU BHALAARE
242	1962	NUVVAA NENAA	MERISE VENDI
243	1962	PATI GOWRAVAME SATIKAANANDAMU(D)	AAKAASAMANDE NEEVUNDUVEMO
244	1962	PATI GOWRAVAME SATIKAANANDAMU(D)	NAVARAAGAMED O NAALO
245	1962	PAVITRA PREMA(D)	CHAKKANI KOMALI MAATALU

246	1962	PAVITRA PREMA(D)	HRUDAYAM AMRUTA SEEMA
247	1962	PAVITRA PREMA(D)	PAALGAARU CHINNAARIVE
248	1962	PELLI TAMBOOLAM	CHAKKANI O JAABILLI
249	1962	PELLI TAMBOOLAM	CHAL BADA MAZAA
250	1962	PELLI TAMBOOLAM	KATHAYENA BRATUKU ILALO
251	1962	PELLI TAMBOOLAM	NITYA VINODAM
252	1962	PELLI TAMBOOLAM	OHO JEEVITAME AANANDAM
253	1962	PRAJA SAKTI(D)	ANDAALA BAALAYE
254	1962	PRAJA SAKTI(D)	LOKAMU
255	1962	RAKTA SAMBANDHAM	EVARO NANNU
256	1962	SAMRAT PRUTHVIRAJ	NEE MAATRU BHOOMIYE
257	1962	SATYABHAMA PARINAYAM(D)	SURYADEVA DAYAAKARAA
258	1962	SIRI SAMPADALU	HOLIDAY
259	1962	SRI VALLI KALYANAM(D)	AANANDA KARAMAINA EENAADE

260	1962	SRI VALLI KALYANAM(D)	DAAHAM TAGGINDI
261	1962	SRI VALLI KALYANAM(D)	HAAI GOORCHU BAALA
262	1962	SRI VALLI KALYANAM(D)	TAAMARAAKUPAI NEETI BINDUVAI
263	1962	SRI VALLI KALYANAM(D)	VIGNA NAAYAKA VILAMBAMU(PAD YAM)
264	1962	SRI VALLI KALYANAM(D)	YENTA DHAIRYAM
265	1962	SWARNA GOWRI	RASAMAYA
266	1962	SWARNA GOWRI	RAAVE NAA CHELIYA
267	1962	SWARNA GOWRI	RAAVO JAABILI
268	1963	ANUBANDHAALU	IDDARU ANUKONI
269	1963	ANURAAGAM	KHUSHI KHUSHIGAA NAATO RAAVE
270	1963	CHADUVUKUNNA AMMAAYILU	OHO CHAKKANI
271	1963	CONISTABLE KOOTURU	CHIGURAAKULA
272	1963	CONISTABLE KOOTURU	CHIGURAAKULA(S AD)

273	1963	CONISTABLE KOOTURU	POOVU VALE
274	1963	CONISTABLE KOOTURU	VAGALA
275	1963	CONISTABLE KOOTURU	VENNELA KELA
276	1963	EDUREETA	OKE MAATA OKEMAATA ADAGANAA
277	1963	EDUREETA	POOVU PUTTAGAANE TAANU
278	1963	EDUREETA	VUNNAVAARIKAN NA MANAM
279	1963	EDUREETA	PANCHARU PANCHARU
280	1963	EEDU JODU	SURYUNI CHUTTU
281	1963	GURUVUNU MINCHINA SHISHYUDU	YE DIVYA LOKAALA
282	1963	GURUVUNU MINCHINA SHISHYUDU	EDEDU JANMALA NUNDI
283	1963	GURUVUNU MINCHINA SHISHYUDU	GURUR BRAHMA
284	1963	GURUVUNU MINCHINA SHISHYUDU	KALUVA REKULA KANULU
285	1963	IRUGU PORUGU	JIGI JIGELUMANU

286	1963	IRUGU PORUGU	SANNAJAAJI
287	1963	IRUGU PORUGU	TOTAKU VACCHINDOKA
288	1963	JNAANESWAR(D)	DEVA NEEVAINAA KARUNINCHAVA
289	1963	MANCHI ROJULU VASTAAYI	MANCHI ROJULOSTAAYI
290	1963	MANCHI ROJULU VASTAAYI	O VAYYARI BHAAMA OKAMAATA
291	1963	MANCHI ROJULU VASTAAYI	VIRISI VIRIYANI KUSUMAALU
292	1963	MOODHA NAMMAKAALU(D)	OKE NAVVU OKE NAAVVU
293	1963	PEMPUDU KOOTURU	JEEVANA RAAGAM
294	1963	PEMPUDU KOOTURU	KANNULA VINDAU
295	1963	PENCHINA PREMA	CHAKKANI MITHILA
296	1963	PENCHINA PREMA	MEDADU UNNA MANUSHULANTA
297	1963	RAJADHI RAJU KATHA(D)	CHILIPI VENNELA
298	1963	RAJADHI RAJU KATHA(D)	VINUVEEDHI JAABILI
299	1963	SAVATI KODUKU	NAALO NINDE CHEEKATI

300	1963	SOMAVARA VRATA MAHATYAM	MADHURA
301	1963	SOMAVARA VRATA MAHATYAM	RAJA RAJA CHANDRAMA
302	1963	TALLI BIDDALU	MANASICCHA NENOKA
303	1963	TALLI BIDDALU	NAGUMOMUNA KALA KALA
304	1963	VIJAYANAGARA VEERAPUTRUNI KATHA(D)	APARA KEETRI NINDI
305	1963	VIJAYANAGARA VEERAPUTRUNI KATHA(D)	DAARINI KAACHITIVELA
306	1963	VISHNU MAAYA	HRUDAYA MANDAARAME(P ADYAM)
307	1963	VISHNU MAAYA	MADHURA RAAGAALA
308	1963	VISHNU MAAYA	PRANAYANI NEEDU
309	1963	VISHNU MAAYA	SEMAMBEGADA(P ADYAM)
310	1964	AADARSA SODARULU(D)	AVANILO TIRIGEDI
311	1964	AADARSA SODARULU(D)	NANU MUDDUGA JOOCHEDU
312	1964	BANGARU TIMMARAJU	BALADARYAMMU NA Remove it if columns are not adjusted DURJANUL

313	1964	BANGARU TIMMARAJU	HREEMKAARAASANA(SLOKAM)
314	1964	BANGARU TIMMARAJU	KODE KAARU
315	1964	BANGARU TIMMARAJU	SRI KARANI PADAABJAMULA(PADYAM)
316	1964	BANGARU TIMMARAJU	SRI VENKATESWARA SUPRABHATAM
317	1964	BANGARU TIMMARAJU	SRIMAD RAMAKANTHA DANDAKAM
318	1964	BHAKTA RAMADASU	ADIGO BHADRAADRI
319	1964	BOBBILI YUDDHAM	SEVALU CHEYYAALE
320	1964	DONGA BANGARAM(D)	MUDDUGA MATADI MOJULO
321	1964	DONGALU DORALU(D)	AADI MANUJUNU GAADHA
322	1964	DONGALU DORALU(D)	GAGANAANA TELE RERAAJA
323	1964	DONGALU DORALU(D)	NAA NEEDA NUVVANI
324	1964	DONGALU DORALU(D)	VEDUKAINADI JEEVITAM
325	1964	DR CHAKRAVARTHI	ONTIGA SAMAYAM

326	1964	GUDI GANTALU	NEELI KANNULA
327	1964	INTI DONGA(D)	KATHAANAAYAK A KALALONE
328	1964	INTI DONGA(D)	O BAVA BAVA VINARAAVA
329	1964	INTI DONGA(D)	PREYASI MUKHAME VELIGE
330	1964	INTI DONGA(D)	UNNA GHANATA NEEKUNNA
331	1964	INTI DONGA(D)	VENNELALE MUCCHATAGA
332	1964	KARNA(D)	EEDI ARPINCHU
333	1964	KARNA(D)	SAHASRA HASTAMMULU
334	1964	KAVALA PILLALU(D)	AAME BALIYAI
335	1964	KAVALA PILLALU(D)	MADHURA NAGARANA
336	1964	MANCHI MANISHI	OHO GULABI
337	1964	MAASTAA RAMMAAYI(D)	MAANAVAATMAY E DAIVA MANDIRAM
338	1964	MAASTAA RAMMAAYI(D)	NAA MANASU DOCHEDU

339	1964	MAASTAA RAMMAAYI(D)	PREMIKULA VINDU
340	1964	MAASTAA RAMMAAYI(D)	SOKAMA SOWKHYAMA
341	1964	MYRAVANA	ATADU SVAAMSA
342	1964	MYRAVANA	RAAMANAAMAM SRIRAMA NAAMAM
343	1964	NAVAGRAHA POOJA MAHIMA	INTA CHERUVALONE
344	1964	NAVAGRAHA POOJA MAHIMA	RAAVANA PATANAM(PADYAM)
345	1964	NAVAGRAHA POOJA MAHIMA	SURYA SOWRYA
346	1964	NAVARATNA KHADGA RAHASYAM(D)	VIRIYELA VIPARITAMAYI
347	1964	PEETALA MEEDA PELLI	MAA TELIVI MAAKU VADALI
348	1964	PEETALA MEEDA PELLI	MUNDADUGU VESINDI
349	1964	PEETALA MEEDA PELLI	PEETALA MEEDA PELLI
350	1964	PEETALA MEEDA PELLI	SURYUNIKI JAABILIKI
351	1964	RAKTA TILAKAM(D)	JAAJI PUVVAI CHALLAGAA

352	1964	RAKTA TILAKAM(D)	PALUMAATA LELA
353	1964	TOTALO PILLA KOTALO RANI	EGIRETI CHINNADAANA
354	1964	TOTALO PILLA KOTALO RANI	KALALO MELAKUVA
355	1964	VANASUNDARI(D)	YELABBHAI PARIHAASAM
356	1964	VEERA SENAPATI(D)	AHAHA AAGU INTA TEKKAA
357	1964	VIVAHA BANDHAM	NEETILONA NINGILONA
358	1965	AADA BRATUKU	AHAA ANADAMU
359	1965	AADA BRATUKU	BUJJI
360	1965	AADA BRATUKU	KANULU
361	1965	AADA BRATUKU	NEEDU KURULA
362	1965	AADA BRATUKU	OMKAARA ROOPINI
363	1965	AADA BRATUKU	TANUVUKENNI GAAYAALAINAA
364	1965	AAKAASA RAAMANNA	DAAGAVULE DAAGAVULE
365	1965	AAKAASA RAAMANNA	OHO CHINNAVAADA

366	1965	ADRUSYA HANTAKUDU(D)	BHOOTAKAM CHELUNI NATANA
367	1965	ADRUSYA HANTAKUDU(D)	JAANAVULE NERA JAANAVULE
368	1965	ADRUSYA HANTAKUDU(D)	KANEETI MAYAMURA
369	1965	ANDI ANDANI PREMA(D)	CHINNI KRISHNUDASINCH U
370	1965	ANDI ANDANI PREMA(D)	OOHALEVO MADILONA
371	1965	ANDI ANDANI PREMA(D)	RAAVAMMA MARI MRAAVAMMA
372	1965	ANDI ANDANI PREMA(D)	VANITALILA MAGANIVADDA
373	1965	BHEEMA PRATIGNA(D)	PAALAVENNELA JAGAMUNA
374	1965	CHADUVUKUNNA BHAARYA	CHELEE NEESOGASU
375	1965	CHADUVUKUNNA BHAARYA	JEEVITAME VINTA
376	1965	CHADUVUKUNNA BHAARYA	MAATI MAATIKI
377	1965	CHANDRAHASA	MAATAA MARAKATASYAA MAA(STROTRAM)
378	1965	DEVATA	BHALAARE DHEERUDU

379	1965	ILLAALU	ANDAMANTE NUVVE
380	1965	ILLAALU	PO PO PO RA RA RA NUVVU
381	1965	KATHANAYAKUDU KATHA(D)	RANIVO NERAJAANAVO
382	1965	MARANI MANASAULU(D)	HRUDAYAM NINU PILICHE
383	1965	MARANI MANASAULU(D)	KALASINA MANASULU
384	1965	PAKKALO BALLEM	TELUSU YEMO ANDAANIKI
385	1965	PANDAVA VANAVASAM	O KAMALAANANAA
386	1965	PRACHANDA BHAIRAVI	NAALONI ANDAALANNI NEEKOSAME
387	1965	PREMINCHI CHOODU	ADI OKA IDILE
388	1965	PREMINCHI CHOODU	MEDA MEEDA
389	1965	PREMINCHI CHOODU	MEE ANDAALA CHETULU
390	1965	PREMINCHI CHOODU	VENNELA REYI
391	1965	PREMINCHI PELLI CHESUKO(D)	KANNULA MERUPULA
392	1965	SATI SAKKUBAI	ASATOMA

393	1965	SATI SAKKUBAI	BAADHALE TEEREGA
394	1965	SATI SAKKUBAI	CHITTA PARISUDDHITO
395	1965	SATI SAKKUBAI	DAARUKA VANA
396	1965	SATI SAKKUBAI	KANALE HIRANYA KASIPU
397	1965	SATI SAKKUBAI	KANALI HIRANYA KASYAPUDU
398	1965	SINDBAD ALI BABA ALLADDIN(D)	RANIVO NERAJAANAV
399	1965	SIVARATRI MAHATYAM(D)	NAVVE VENNELA REYI
400	1965	SIVARATRI MAHATYAM(D)	PRIYA MOHINI KANULALO
401	1965	SRI SIMHACHALA KSETRA MAHIMA	JAYAHE
402	1965	SRI SIMHACHALA KSETRA MAHIMA	RAAVOYI RAAJA
403	1965	SUMANGALI	YEVEVO CHILIP
404	1965	TENE MANASULU	PURUSHUDU
405	1965	TENE MANASULU	YEM YENDUKANI
406	1965	TODU NEEDA	VALAPULONI

407	1965	VIJAYA SIMHA	OU NANNAAVO
408	1966	AAME EVARU	DIKI RIKI DIKI RIKI
409	1966	AAME EVARU	NEEVU CHOOSE CHOOPULO
410	1966	AATA BOMMALU	NUVVU NENU JATTU
411	1966	ADAVI PILLA(D)	MURIPINCHE BHAAMA YELE
412	1966	ADAVI PILLA(D)	SNEHAMTO MANASU
413	1966	ADAVI YODHUDU(D)	AAMANI KOYILA
\414	1966	ADUGU JAADALU	NAA CHELI KANNULA
415	1966	BHAKTA POTANA	ALA VAIKUNTHA PURAMBULO
416	1966	BHAKTA POTANA	AMBA NAVAAMBUJOJW ALA
417	1966	BHAKTA POTANA	JAYAMU JAYAMU MANAKU
418	1966	BHAKTA POTANA	KAATUKA KANTINEERU
419	1966	BHAKTA POTANA	NEE DAYA RAADA

420	1966	BHAKTA POTANA	PALIKEDIDI BHAAGAVATAMA TA
421	1966	BHAKTA POTANA	PALIKEDIDI BHAAGAVATAMA TA(PADYAM)
422	1966	BHAKTA POTANA	PATTI VIDUVA RAADU
423	1966	BHAKTA POTANA	SARASWATI NAMASTUBHYAM (SLOKAM)
424	1966	BHAKTA POTANA	SARVA MANGALA NAAMA
425	1966	BHAKTA POTANA	SARADA NEERADENDU GHANA
426	1966	BHAKTA POTANA	SRAVANA MEGHALU
427	1966	BHAKTA POTANA	SREE KAIVALYA PADAMBU(PADYA M)
428	1966	BHAKTA POTANA	SREEMAN MAHA
429	1966	BHOOLOKAMLO YAMLOKAM	ANDUKO ANDISTANURA
430	1966	BHOOLOKAMLO YAMLOKAM	NAMOSTUTE(SLO KAM)
431	1966	DOCTOR ANAND	MUSUGU

432	1966	EVARA STREE(D)	POOJALU PANDINA SUBHAVELA
433	1966	KANNE PILLA(D)	EENADU NEEVU TODU
434	1966	KANNE PILLA(D)	JAAV RE JAAV
435	1966	KATTI POTU(D)	RAAGAALA TELINCHUMA
436	1966	LETA MANASULU	ANDAALA CHELIKAADAA(SAD)
437	1966	LETA MANASULU	ANDAALA OH CHILAKA
438	1966	LETA MANASULU	EE PUVVULALO
439	1966	LETA MANASULU	HELLO MADAM
440	1966	LOGUTTU PERUMALLAKERUKA	DAARI KAACHI VEELU
441	1966	MANASE MANDIRAMU	TALACHINADE
442	1966	MANGALA SUTRAM	ANDAALA CHINNADAANI
443	1966	MANGALA SUTRAM	BALE BALE POSUKOLU
444	1966	MANGALA SUTRAM	IDI CHEEKATI JEEVITAM

445	1966	MONAGAALLAKU MONAGAADU	AHAHA CHOODU ANDAMU
446	1966	MONAGAALLAKU MONAGAADU	ANDAALA BOMMALAAGA
447	1966	MONAGAALLAKU MONAGAADU	NENUNNADI NEELONE
448	1966	MONAGAALLAKU MONAGAADU	VACCHAAME NEEKOSAM
449	1966	PAADUKA PATTAABHISHEKAM	OHO NAA PREYASI
450	1966	PAADUKA PATTAABHISHEKAM	PILINCHITI NENU(PADYAM)
451	1966	PAADUKA PATTAABHISHEKAM	SUGUNABHI RAAMUNI(PADYAM)
452	1966	PALNAATI YUDDHAM	TEEYANI TOLIREYI
453	1966	POTTI PLEADARU	OOGENU MNANASU
454	1966	SERVER SUNDARAM(D)	POOTA POOCHE HRUDAYAM
455	1966	SREE KRISHNA PANDAVEEYAMU	AA ELANAGAA
456	1966	SREE KRISHNA PANDAVEEYAMU	ANIKILI SEPPALEDU
457	1966	SREE KRISHNA PANDAVEEYAMU	EMITAYAA NEE LEELA

458	1966	SREE KRISHNA PANDAVEEYAMU	KRISHNA YADUBHOOSHANAA
459	1966	SREE KRISHNA PANDAVEEYAMU	NALLANI VAADU
460	1966	SREE KRISHNA PANDAVEEYAMU	TAGU NEE CHAKRI
461	1966	SREE KRISHNA PANDAVEEYAMU	TALAMANAKA
462	1966	SRIMATI	ARUNAM(SLOKAM)
463	1966	VIJAYA SANKHAM	TUNTARI CHINNA VAADA
464	1967	CHIKKADU DORAKADU	AURA VEERAADHI VEERA
465	1967	CHIKKADU DORAKADU	VIRISINA & PAGATI POOTA
466	1967	DEVUNI GELICHINA MANAVUDU	CHAKKALIGILI PETTALANI
467	1967	DEVUNI GELICHINA MANAVUDU	CHELI KADALI RAAVE
468	1967	DHANAME PRAPANCHA LEELA(D)	AMMA AMMA ANE
469	1967	DHANAME PRAPANCHA LEELA(D)	LOKAMANTA MOHANA
470	1967	KALACHAKRAM(D)	MAGUVALA HRUDAYAM

471	1967	KONTE PILLA(D)	MOHAMO MAIKAMO
472	1967	KONTE PILLA(D)	SUKHAPADUTA EE ILALO
473	1967	MULLA KIREETAM(D)	CHALLANI PILUPU
474	1967	PATTUKUNTE PADIVELU	SWAAGATAM SUSWAAGATA
475	1967	PEDDA AKKAYYA	PICNIC PICNIC
476	1967	PINNI	CHANEETI LONA
477	1967	PINNI	KALAVAALI
478	1967	PREMALO PRAMADAM	NAMME VAARE NAMMAKAPOTE
479	1967	PREMALO PRAMADAM	VALAPE
480	1967	PRIVATE MASTARU	EKKADA UNTAAVO
481	1967	RANGULA RATNAM	KANNULA DAAGINA
482	1967	SAKSHI	DAYALEDAA
483	1967	SAKSHI	GUNAKAARI GUNNAMMA
484	1967	SATI SUMATI	HAAYI VEEDI

485	1967	SATYAME JAYAM	NEEVE NENU
486	1967	SIVA LEELALU(D)	MUDITA MEEDA KORIKACHE
487	1967	SRI SRI MARYADA RAMANNA	EMI EE VINTA MOHAMU
488	1967	SRI KRISHNA MAHIMA(D)	ACHYUTAM KESAVAM(SLOKA M)
489	1967	SRI KRISHNA MAHIMA(D)	DEVUNI SANNIDHI
490	1967	SRI KRISHNA MAHIMA(D)	ENNI NAALLA KENNAALLAKU
491	1967	SRI KRISHNA MAHIMA(D)	HEY DWAARAKAA NAADHA
492	1967	SRI KRISHNA MAHIMA(D)	KROORAMAINA DAARIDRYAMUTO
493	1967	SRI KRISHNA MAHIMA(D)	MAAYA MAADHAVA GOPAALA
494	1967	UPAYAMLO APAYAM	PADAARU GADICHI
495	1967	VASANTA SENA	OHO VASANTA YAMINI
496	1968	AMAYAKUDU	ANUKONNA IDI
497	1968	AMAYAKUDU	BOMMANU GEESAAVU

498	1968	ANTULENI HANTAKUDU(D)	O AMMAAYI
499	1968	ASADHYUDU	CHITTEMMAA CHINNAMMAA
500	1968	ASADHYUDU	ILAA ILAA UNTUNNADI
501	1968	ATTAGARU KOTTA KODALU	DEVAA LOKAMULONI
502	1968	ATTAGARU KOTTA KODALU	NUVVU LENIDE
503	1968	BHARYA	AYYAYYO AYYO
504	1968	CHALLANI NEEDA	ANAGANAGAA
505	1968	CHELLELI KOSAM	KANNEETI KONETILONA
506	1968	CHELLELI KOSAM	NIJAANNI NAMMADU LOKAM
507	1968	CHELLELI KOSAM	VINTAANANTE PADATAA
508	1968	CHUTTARIKAALU	YEMITO EE VINTA
509	1968	CIRCAR EXPRESS	CHELI KANULE
510	1968	DEVUDICCHINA BHARTA	AA DEVUDICCHINA
511	1968	DEVUDICCHINA BHARTA	PARUVAALA VAAGULO

512	1968	DEVUDICCHINA BHARTA	RAAVEME PILLAA
513	1968	EVARU MONAGAADU	JINUKADI JINUKADI
514	1968	EVARU MONAGAADU	KANULE NEDE
515	1968	EVARU MONAGAADU	LALLA LALALLA UNNAANU
516	1968	EVARU MONAGAADU	MANASAARA
517	1968	GALATA PELLILLU(D)	MOHAMULU SAAGE
518	1968	GALATA PELLILLU(D)	O PAAPA NEEKAMMA
519	1968	GALATA PELLILLU(D)	RANDI RAARANDOI
520	1968	GALATA PELLILLU(D)	SWAAGATAM GHANA SWAAGATAM
521	1968	JEEVITAALU	PUTTEVU NEDU
522	1968	KALASINA MANASULU	POTAAVANTE PILLAA
523	1968	KUMKUMA BHARANI	NAYAA JAMAANAA GAYAA
524	1968	KUMKUMA BHARANI	VAAKILI MOOSI

525	1968	LAKSHMI NIVAASAM	CHEYI CHEYI KALUPU
526	1968	LAKSHMI NIVAASAM	OHO VOORINCHE AMMAAYI
527	1968	MANA SAMSAARAM	GAAYAPADINA PREMIKA
528	1968	MANA SAMSAARAM	MY DEAR VAYYAARI
529	1968	NADAMANTRAPU SIRI	NEE CHALLANI MANASU
530	1968	PALA MANASULU	IDE SAMAADHAANAM
531	1968	PALA MANASULU	PALAVANKA SEEMALO
532	1968	PELLI ROJU	AANAATI CHELIMI OKA KALA
533	1968	PELLI ROJU	ADUGUDAAMANI UNDI
534	1968	PELLI ROJU	AHA YEGIREGIRI PADUTONDI
535	1968	PELLI ROJU	JEEVITAANA MARUVALEMU
536	1968	PELLI ROJU	MAGUVALA VALALO
537	1968	PELLI ROJU	PELLIVAARAMAN DI AADA

538	1968	RAJAYOGAM	EE SAMYAM EMITO
539	1968	RANA BHERI	VALAPU KOWGILILO
540	1968	TALLI PREMA	LEDA
541	1968	TALLI PREMA	NINNA
542	1968	TALLI PREMA	TALLI
543	1968	VEERAANJANEYA	HIMSAKANDA ETC(PADYAMS)
544	1968	VEERAANJANEYA	INTAKANNA MADHURAMAINA
545	1968	VEERAANJANEYA	NAVA RAAGAME
546	1968	VEERAANJANEYA	RAAMA NAAMAME
547	1968	VEERAANJANEYA	SRI KRISHNA KRISHNA
548	1968	VIDHI(D)	MATI POYE NEEKAI
549	1968	VIDHI(D)	SAMAYAM PRASAANTA
550	1968	VIDHI(D)	SILA AINANU PHALAMAINANU
551	1969	AADARSA PELLILLU(D)	KALALU GAANCHI

552	1969	KARPOORA HAARATI	KALASINA HRUDAYAALALONA
553	1969	LOVE IN ANDHRA	ANDAM UNNADI
554	1969	LOVE IN ANDHRA	EEMMA EEMMA EEMMAA
555	1969	LOVE IN ANDHRA	PO PO POMMANTE
556	1969	MOOGA NOMU	OORU MAARINAA UNIKI MAARUNNA
557	1969	NAATAKAALA RAYUDU	NALABHAIKI
558	1969	PREMA KAANUKA	OKKA CHELI
559	1969	SAPTA SWARAALU	HAAYIGAA PAADANAA
560	1969	SAPTA SWARAALU	YAAKUNBENDU(SLOKAM)
561	1969	SATTEKAALAPU SATTEYYA	MUDDU MUDDU NEEVU
562	1969	SATTEKAALAPU SATTEYYA	MUDDU MUDDU NAVVU -BIT
563	1969	TAARA SASAANKAMU	PREMA YANA NETTIDO(PADYAM)
564	1969	TAARA SASAANKAMU	VANDE JANANI

565	1970	AKHANDUDU	O HAMSANADALA DAANAA
566	1970	AKHANDUDU	OYAMMO INTA KOPAM
567	1970	AKHANDUDU	RAARA RAMMANTE RAAVELA
568	1970	AMMA KOSAM	ADE
569	1970	DESAMANTE MANUSHULOI	DEVA KARUNAAMAYA
570	1970	DESAMANTE MANUSHULOI	DEVAA
571	1970	SAMBARAALA RAAMBABU	KANNULE
572	1970	YAMALOKAPU GOODHACHAARI	PHALAMU KAADIDI(PADYAM)
573	1970	YAMALOKAPU GOODHACHAARI	A AH HA PILACHINADI
574	1970	YAMALOKAPU GOODHACHAARI	NAA DESAME
575	1971	ADAVI VEERULU	JO JO CHINNAARI
576	1971	AANANDA NILAYAM	EE KANNE GULAABI
577	1971	CHELLELI KAAPURAM	EE DAARI NAA SWAAMY

578	1971	KATTIKI KANKANAM	GAPPAM KATTULU
579	1971	SATI ANASUYA	GANGAA DHAARYA(PADYA M)
580	1971	SATI ANASUYA	MANCHI MANASUNU
581	1971	SATI ANASUYA	OH CHELI VIDUVALENE
582	1971	SRI VENKATESWARA VAIBHAVAM	PARITRAANAAYA SAADHOONAAM
583	1971	SREE KRISHNA DEVARAYALU(D)	AKHILA SASTRAASTRA
584	1971	SREE KRISHNA DEVARAYALU(D)	KALAI NATBUTA
585	1971	SREE KRISHNA DEVARAYALU(D)	KRISHNA SREEKARA
586	1971	SREE KRISHNA DEVARAYALU(D)	PALU JANMALA
587	1971	TALLINI MINCHINA TALLI(D)	EESWARUDU EE LOKAANIKI
588	1972	ABBAIGAARU AMMAYIGAARU	SUBHADRAARJUN EEYAM
589	1972	BEEDALA PAATLU	DABBULONE
590	1972	MAA INTI KODALU	MADHUVULONI MAHIMA
591	1972	MENAKODALU	AASALU VIRISE

592	1972	SABASH BABY	NEELO HRUDAYAM
593	1972	SAMPOORNA RAMAYANAM	DHANUJUNI
594	1972	SAMPOORNA RAMAYANAM	HAARATI
595	1972	SAMPOORNA RAMAYANAM	MAARTAANDU GHANA TEJA
596	1972	SAMPOORNA RAMAYANAM	SAKALA JAGAJJAALA
597	1972	SAMPOORNA RAMAYANAM	SEETAA RAAMULA KALYAANAM
598	1972	SAMPOORNA RAMAYANAM	SREE ANJANEYAM
599	1972	SAMPOORNA RAMAYANAM	VANDE VAANARA
600	1972	SAMPOORNA RAMAYANAM	VEDALENU KODANDA PAANI-1
601	1972	SAMPOORNA RAMAYANAM	VEDALENU KODANDA PAANI-2
602	1972	SAMPOORNA RAMAYANAM	VEDALENU KODANDA PAANI-3
603	1972	SAMPOORNA RAMAYANAM	VEDALENU KODANDA PAANI-4
604	1972	TIRUPATI-KANYAAKUMAARI YAATRA(D)	TIRUPATI PAI

605	1974	INTINTI KATHA	RAMANI MUDDULA
606	1974	KRISHNA VENI	HEY JANANI KRISHNAVENI
607	1975	MAYA MACHINDRA	RAAMA SUGUNA DHAAMA
608	1975	SRI RAMANAJANEYA YUDDHAM	RAAMA SUGUNA DHAAMA
609	1976	DHARMA NIRNAYAM	DASARATHA VARA
610	1976	SEETHA KALYAANAM	ANTAA RAAMAMAYAM
611	1976	SEETHA KALYAANAM	INVAMSA JALAJAATA
612	1976	SEETHA KALYAANAM	JAANAKI RAAMULA
613	1976	SEETHA KALYAANAM	KALYAANAM CHOODAM
614	1976	SEETHA KALYAANAM	LAKSHMEEM KSHEERA
615	1976	SEETHA KALYAANAM	MAA JAANAKI
616	1976	SEETHA KALYAANAM	MAHAA VISHNUVU
617	1976	SEETHA KALYAANAM	MUNIVENTA VANASEEMA
618	1976	SEETHA KALYAANAM	NAA TANDRI(PADYAM)

619	1976	SEETHA KALYAANAM	PARAMA PAAVANAMAINA
620	1976	SEETHA KALYAANAM	RAGHU KULA
621	1976	SEETHA KALYAANAM	RAAMA CHANDRAAYA
622	1976	SEETHA KALYAANAM	SEETAA RAAMULA SUBHA CHARITAM
623	1976	SEETHA KALYAANAM	SEETAMMA VIHARINCHU
624	1976	SEETHA KALYAANAM	SUDDHA LAKSHMEE MOKSHA(SLOKAM)
625	1977	CHAKRA DHAARI	IDE PRATI JEEVIKI
626	1977	KURUKSHETRAMU	VASIGA BHAAMA
627	1977	MANAVADI KOSAM	NEEKU NENU KAAVAALI
628	1977	MANCHI ROJU	CHEPPAALANUND I
629	1977	MANCHI ROJU	NEE KOSAMANI
630	1977	SNEHAM	EGARESINA GAALI PATAALU
631	1977	TARAM MAARINDI	EDI SATYAM

632	1978	GORANTA DEEPAM	CHAL MOHANA RANGA
633	1978	GORANTA DEEPAM	CHEERA MAARCHI
634	1978	GORANTA DEEPAM	KAVITALU
635	1978	GORANTA DEEPAM	POOLU TAAKINANTA
636	1978	KARUNAMAYUDU	PARA LOKAMANDUNNA
637	1978	SWAMY AYYAPPA(D)	GURU BRAHMAM
638	1978	SWAMY AYYAPPA(D)	POOLA VANAMANDU
639	979	NAGNA SATYAM	BANGAARAM VANNE KOSAM
640	1979	SRI TIRUPATI VENKATESWARA KALYANAM	SUPRABHAATAM
641	1980	CHUKKALLO CHANDRUDU	HARI OM
642	1980	CHUKKALLO CHANDRUDU	RAAMA SUGUNA DHAAMA
643	1980	MADANA MANJARI	SEVALONI AANANDAM
644	1980	SWAPNA	SRIRASTU ABBAYI
645	1981	TYAAGAYYA	BHAJA GOVINDAM

646	1982	MANTRAALAYA SREE RAGHAVENDRA VAIBHAVAMU	KARUNA DEEPAM
647	1982	MANTRAALAYA SREE RAGHAVENDRA VAIBHAVAMU	MANASUKU NEMMADI
648	1982	PATNAM VACCHINA PATIVRTALU	SANKARAA GANGAADHARAA
649	1983	KOKILAMMA	MADHURAM MADHURAM
650	1988	SRIDEVI KAAMAAKSHI KATAAKSHAM	SRI SARADA DEVI
651	1990	MRUTYUM JAYUDU	BAALA BHAASKARUDU
652	1990	MRUTYUM JAYUDU	SIVUNI CHOOCHEDAVAA

Telugu songs of PBS based on Classical Ragas:

S. No	Song	Raaga	Movie
1	'Aaanaati Chelimi Oka Kala'	Aabheri-Bhimpalaas	Pelli Roju
2	'Manasuloni Korika'	Kalyani	Bheeshma
3	'Poovu Vale Virabooyvale	Kaanada	Constable Kooturu
4	'Talachinade Jariginada'	Keeravani	Manase Mandiram
5	'Kannulu Daachina Anuraagam'	Gaurimanohari	Rangularatnam
6	'Neevuchuse Chupulo Ennenni'	Chandrakos	Aame Evaru

7	‘Ooorumaarina Uniki Maaruna’	Chaarukesa	Mooga Nomu
8	‘Manasu Manasulo’	Patadeep	Rangularatnam
9	‘Evevo Chilipi Talapu Lolukuchunnavi’	Pahaad	Sumangali
10	‘Jeevitana Maruvalemu Oke Roju’	Bhageswari	Pelli Roju
11	‘Andaaluchindu Seemalo’	Bhageswari	Raajanandini
12	‘Emi Ramakadha’	Dwijaavanti+Sahan a	Bhakta Sabari
13	‘Oho Gulaabi Baala’	Yaman	Manchi Manishi
14	‘Anuraaga Seema Manameludaama’	Raageswari	Kanakadurga Puja
15	‘Neetilona Ningilona’	Shankarabharanam	Vivaahabandham
16	‘Anadaala O Chiluka Anduko Naa’	Shankarabharanam	Letha Manasulu
17	‘Neelikannula Needalalona’	Sindhubhairavi	Gudi Gantalu
18	‘Sri Raghuram Jaya Raghuram’	Hamsadhwani	Shanti Nivasam
19	‘Deva Deva Parandhama’	Hindola	Seetha Ramakalyanam

The reasons for PBS not becoming as much popular in Telugu field as in Kannada or Tamil fields:

Feeble minds can easily say that Ghantasala who was the reigning king of Telugu film field, did not allow PBS to shine. But if we adopt scientific approach, i.e., a systematic, unbiased and logical approach, the available evidence tells us that Ghantasala always encouraged the younger singers, both male and female, by patting on their back and giving chances to them as a renowned music composer. With regard to PBS, he had a soft corner for

him and encouraged him when he started playback singing. He used to affectionately call him 'Tammudu' ('Tammudu' in Telugu means younger brother). He openly appreciated some of the songs sung by PBS, like 'Oho Gulabi Baala' and 'Nilave ennidam nerungathe', and made him sing excellent songs in movies like "Gudigantalu", and "Shantinivasam". In Kannada too, he made PBS sing beautiful songs.

Then what could be the reason?

1. Indian movies in general and Southern Indian movies in particular are film star–oriented and are based on the personality and popularity of the heroes. In the Kannada field, PBS sang for the much-acclaimed matinee idol for about 21 years. Ardent fans of Raj Kumar automatically became ardent fans of PBS too. In Tamil field too, PBS sang for the popular hero Gemini Ganesan for about 16 years and automatically became popular.

   In the Telugu field, Ghantasala was the voice of the most popular heroes N.T. RamaRao (NTR) and Akkineni Nageswara Rao (ANR) for about three decades. Being an expert in the idiolects of NTR as well as ANR, he mesmerised Telugu audience by singing thousands of songs which were pictured on those heroes. All this went to the extent that the audience, producers as well as the heroes did not accept any singer other than Ghantasala even though the songs sung for the respective heroes by PBS became popular, i.e., songs like 'Evariki Evaru Kaapala' and 'Bujji Bujji Paapayi' for NTR, and 'Vennela Reyi', 'Meda Meeda Meda Katti', 'Adi Oka Idi Le' for ANR.

2. T.L.Kanta Rao played roles in mythological movies and period dramas based on fictitious kings and

magicians, princes and princesses.He was the choice of producers and directors next only to N.T. Rama Rao. In some movies, Ghantasala sang for him and in some other movies PBS did, but Kanta Rao wasn't accepted as a hero in social movies. As the number of mythological/period dramas produced came down, PBS' chances also dwindled.

3. Another handsome hero who shone like a star on the firmament of Telugu cinema was Haranath Raju. He played mythological roles, those of Rama, Krishna and Vishnu, the roles of princes in movies like "Chandrahasa" and "Madana KamaRaju Katha", and got the appreciation of the audience by his presentable appearance as well as acting skills. Though Ghantasala sang a few melodious songs for Haranath, PBS' voice suited the handsome hero and he sang popular songs like 'Andaala O Chiluka', 'Neeli Meghamaalavo' and 'Hello Madam Satyabhama'. The melodious and meaningful padyams in movies like "Bhishma" got him much acclaim from the audience. But unfortunately, the handsome hero got addicted to heavy drinking and ruined his bright career in the movies. Had Haranath continued to be at the top as a hero, PBS would have made a niche for himself in the hearts of the Telugus.

4. When S.P. Balasubrahmanyam (S.P. Balu) entered the Southern Indian film field in the mid 1960's, he was just 20 years old-about 20 years younger than PBS. With his youthful vigour, useful marketing skills, admirable grasping abilities and excellent mimicry skills, SPB 's star rose quickly and steadily on the firmament of the Southern Indian Cinema. With his deft mimicry skills, he could sing for old heroes like ANR and NTR, young heroes like Krishna and Sobhan Babu, and comedians like

Allu Ramalingiah and Rajubabu; with his quick grasping skills he used the 'Bani' of Ghantasala, of PBS and of Madhavapeddi whichever was appropriate for the song. (I may add here that mimicry and grasping skills are important for a playback singer) In this manner, SPB captured the Telugu, the Tamil and even the Kannada film industries. The advent of SPB, along with other factors also gave a big blow to PBS.

Notes

1. Taken from T.M. Krishna's 'A Southern Music: The Karnatic Story

2. Taken from Ranganath Nandyal's 'The Song and Its Sweep' The Hindu, 21 June, 2013.

3. Ibid

4. Taken from my sister K. Vijayalakshmi's and Ramesh Panchakarla's lists

With Ghantasala

With S. Rajeswara Rao

With Master Venu

With T.V Raju

M.S.Vishwanathan

Ghantasala with K.V. Mahadevan

CHAPTER 5

MANOHARA MALAYALAM

"Even though He created so many wonders in the world, the most wonderful creation of Him is Music."

-Subrahmanya Bharati[1]

In the year 1955, PBS entered the Malayalam film field through the movie "Puthra Dharmam" with music composed by P.S. Diwakar. In no time, he was able to create a niche for himself in Malayalam. Some of his songs that stood the test of times and beyond in Malayalam were 'Maha Thyagame' from Harichandra, 'Katha Parrayaam' from Umma, 'Paavana Bharatha' from Sita, 'Mannavanaayaalum' from Satyabhama, 'Iniyoru Janmamundo' and 'Baliyalla Enikku Vaendathu' from Rebecca, 'Yaatrakkara Povuka Povuka' from the film Ayisha which had music by R.K.Shekhar, A.R.Rahman's father, and his songs for Baburaj, a composer of undying fame, 'Geethe Hrudhaya Sakhi' from Poochchakkanni and 'Inakkuyile Inakkuyile' from Kaattuthulasi.

The only song sung by PBS under Salil Chowdhury's baton 'Raathri Raathri' in the film "Yezhu Raathrigal" fully exploited the possibilities of his deep voice. But his most famous song in Malayalam 'Maamalakalkkappurrathu' came under Baburaj's music direction in the movie Ninnamanninjna Kaalppadugal. Even today, it is practically the anthem of Malayalees living away from their motherland longing to go back and living in dreams contemplating its many graces.[2]

Some PBS' most melodious Malayalam songs are ut infra[3]:

Maha Thyaagame *from* **Harischandra (1955)**
This was his first Malayalam movie song. The clarity and almost flawless diction PBS managed to achieve in the song is amazing. Lyrics whereby **Thirunayinarkurichi Madhavan Nair** and music by **B.R. Lakshmanan**.

Udavaale padavale *from* **Unniyarcha (1961)**
Udavaale Padavale plays in the background as Unniyarcha watches her son and Aaromal Chekavar's son practising their weaponry and combat skills, in order to exact her revenge on Chanthu. The scene also clearly captures the inner turmoil of Unniyarcha at the same time. There is a concluding version of this song which starts off with ***Jayabheri Uyarattey***, which is heard as the two young warriors celebrate after having slain Chanthu. Lyricist for this song was P.Bhaskaran and music was composed by K.Raghavan

Kanninaal kaanmathellam *from* **Krishna Kuchela (1961)**
A song in praise of Lord Krishna and his boundless generosity and blessings, picturized on Kuchela's (T.S Muthaiah) family. Lyricist for this song was P.Bhaskaran and the music composer was K.Raghavan

Enthinu neeyiniyum from Christmas Rathri (1961)
Chandanakkinnam *from* **Vidhi Thanna Vilakku (1962)**
Music : V Dakshinamoorthy
Lyrics: P Bhaskaran
A romantic song picturised on Sasi (Sathyan) and Bhavani (Raagini), Vidhi Thanna Vilakku (1962) also one more comedy number beautifully sung by PBS, 'Karakku Company' picturised on SP Pillai and Bahadoor. For this movie music was composed by V. Dakshinamoorthy and the lyricist for this song was P. Bhaskaran.

Maamalakalkkappurathu *from* **Ninamaninja Kaalpaadukal (1963)**

Long before KJ Yesudas's *'Naaleekeratthinte Naattilenikkoru'* from **Thurakkaatha Vaathil** (1970) soothed the homesickness of the Malayali working away from home, there was PBS's happy, peppy, chirpy 'Maamalakalkkappurathu' conjuring up idyllic, nostalgic images of home. This song from Ninamaninja Kaalpaadukal was created by the legendary **P Bhaskaran** – **M.S .Baburaj** combination. Interestingly, *'Naaleekeratthinte'* was also written by Bhaskaran Master (tuned by **K Raghavan Master**).

Yatrakkaara *from* **Ayisha (1964)**

Heard/rendered in the background during a train journey, which also forms the moment where Bashir (Prem Nazir) meets Ayisha (Sasirekha) who is married to Aboobacker Sahib (Sathyan). The lyricist for this song was Vayalar and the music composer was R. K. Sekhar.

Inakkuyile *from* **Kaattuthulasi (1964)**

Most songs of PBS fall into the serious/philosophical/sad/romantic category. Movies like Rebecca, Poochakkanni and Baalyakaalasakhi have many such songs. But the song Inakkuyile from **Kaattuthulasi** (1964) is the one which haunts every music lover. You can sense the desperation of the lover for his beloved, fearing the worst, right from the initial heart-wrenching plea *'Thulasee... Vili Kelkkoo'* and Sathyan's presence on screen is a bonus.

Amrutam pakarnna Rathri *from* **Vidhi (1968)**

Vidhi (1968) was the Malayalam-dubbed version of Taqdeer (1967) had in place of its classic 'Jab Jab Bahar aaye', our own Amrutam Pakarunna Rathri in three versions. The final

version has PB Srinivas, S Janaki and KJ Yesudas rendering the song in all its emotional fullness.
The Malayalam – dubbed version had S Janaki singing for Farida Jalal, P B Srinivas lends his voice to the young actor while Dr KJ Yesudas' part is reserved for Bharat Bhushan. If S Janaki and PB Srinivas brings on the joi-de-vivre of love in their vocals, its longing, separation and pain that is echoed in Dr KJ yesudas' voice. PB Srinivas' vocals are heavenly in this verse.

Devayani, Devayani *from* Aparadhini (1968)

One of those very common instances from old Malayalam films which have theatre acts incorporated for the sake of a song. Here, Sathyan as Rajagopalan dreams himself to be Kacha in the Kacha-Devayani play that he is watching. The lyricist was P. Bhaskaran and the music was composed by M.B. Srinivasan.

Brucelee Kunjallayo *from* Raju Rahim (1978)

Picturised on Raju – Rahim (Prem Nazir and KP Ummer) and Bahadoor, this song, according to me was the the last song sung by PBS for Malayalam movies. The Music composer for this movie was M.K. Arjunan and the lyricist for the song was R.K. Damodaran

Jheel Kinaare *from* Thadaakam (1982)
Dr. PBS was known to be a prolific writer in several languages. This Hindi song from the **IV Sasi** hit **Thadaakam (1982)** is captivating in the voice of S. Janaki with music by the talented AT Ummer. The picturisation strongly resembles the song sequence 'Ye chaand sa roshan chehraa' from the Shammi Kapoor-Sharmila Tagore mega-hit "Kashmir Ki Kali."

With S.P. Balasubramanyam

With K.J. Yesudas

CHAPTER 6
ENTICING ENGLISH

Being a polyglot, PBS wrote poetry in English. We have seen how the young PBS attained command over the English Language by mugging up the entire dictionary of English, and as a result he was nicknamed as 'the Walking Dictionary'. His prominent works in English are "Lovely Love Songs" and "White Shadows".

White Shadows:

This collection of poems by PBS comprises poems of philosophical depth though those look simple and comparable to those Telugu poems of Sri Sri in blank verse. The collocations are thought provoking. Some of those lines are quoted below[1]:

From the poem "Ending is the Beginning"

"Smiling tears
Weeping smiles
Burning feelings
Turbulent dreams
Teach philosophy!"

From the poem "Minds bewildered

Cross horizons
Searching for peace
Reaching new planets
Inventing old truths"

From the poem "Mad Hounds"

"Human stupidity
Knows no bounds

Men chase men
Like mad hounds
Trying to catch
Their own shadows
They lose themselves
Todays and Tomorrows"

From the poem "From the Right side"

"Man runs
After time
Time runs after man
Man misses
Flying time"

From the poem "Nonchalant Time

Treats praise and blame
With no difference
With no preference"

From the poem" Sweet and Bitter"

Reminiscences
Sweet and bitter
Reverberate
In the valley of nostalgic thoughts

From the poem "Gather Your Tears"

"Stop for a while
Move on-
Red signals
Give way to
Green signals!
Traffic flows
Endlessly!

Obstacles
Disappear!
Time marches on!
Your aims
Lead you
Towards the goals!
Goals are
Countless
More than
Ambitions!"

"A devout Singer-Poet believing especially in Melody and Expression, with a flair for languages. A creative and innovative compositor of poems and melodies."

- P.B. Srinivos about himself[2]

Having been excited about the unprecedented event of Neil Armstrong's Landing on the Moon, P.B. Srinivos – using his philosophical as well as scientific knowledge – wrote two songs titled "Man to Moon" and "Moon to God" and sang them along with S. Janaki, which were brought out in record form later. The records were launched in Philadelphia, U.S.A. After listening to the records, the then President of the U.S.A. Richard Nixon and Neil Armstrong sent letters of appreciation to PBS.

I Side - Man to Moon[3]

Man has set his foot on moon
Moon is now but Dehra Doon
Armstrong is n't mere Armstrong
He is mind strong and Aimstrong
Aldrin is THE ANOTHER MAN
Who too walked on Moon and ran
In the Mother-ship seated
Collins is the third who said
"Moon is no more far from Earth

We can travel in her berth
And can go to Planet Mars!
With no need of hungry wars!"
Lucky is this three-some crew
To the skies its repute grew;
Mankind should be proud of this
"Aim of Moon" that failed to miss
What a Glory! What a thrill!
Way is there when there is Will
To the countless shining Stars
Man can go in wingless cars
Man is now a flying bird
Heaven's voice he has heard
So much space is found in SPACE
Every problem man can face
Man is having helping TIME
To be lazy is now crime!
Man should aim at and explore
Unknown planets more and more

II Side - Moon to God

After landing on the Mars
Clay will become golden bars!
From the Mars to Mercury
Man will fly sans injury
Jupiter will be the next
Man will read him as a text
Venus will join (in) the list
To give a romantic twist
Then will Saturn have his turn
And will make the man return
Closing all the doors to Sun
Going where - to is no fun!
Sun will never cease to burn
Hence is not fit for sojourn
Having seen all these planets

All of which are big magnets
Man will acquire rare powers
Stones will change into flowers!
All his powers Man will use
But undoubtedly refuse
To use them for destruction
His goal being 'Construction'
Everything will be sappy
Every life will be happy!
Then there will be no sorrow
From no one will one borrow
There will be no need for fraud
Man will go through 'Good' to God
Man will go alive to God.

Song's Structure – Meaning[4]

The song starts with 'C', meaning that the pitch is the key 'One'. It denotes 'Earth' in this context. Then, it changes from key 1 to 1½ (i.e. C--->1½, key changes to 'C sharp') denoting the 'Space'. Then it continues and reaches Two ('C sharp to D'). Here number Two denotes the 'Moon'. Even as per numerology number two denotes the Moon. So the song has been structured in such a way that it travels from One the Earth and touches the moon, which is Two.

In the next side of the record disc, the song starts from Two and comes back to 1½ i.e through space (1½ refers to the space) and reaches back to Earth.
This indicates the historical journey of man to moon and his safe return to earth, a remarkable achievement.

Another interesting thing about the song is that it is sung by a male singer till the line "to read Jupiter as a book", which is the voice of PBS. The point in which the song starts about planet Venus (Planet that denotes Beauty) the female voice takes over, which is S.Janaki.

More appropriately when the song starts about Saturn the rhythm decreases gradually and goes in Misrum Dvani. The slow Dvani matches its Sanskrit name aptly.

In Sanskrit Saturn is called Sanaicharya meaning one who moves very slowly. It is significant that the rhythm also changes to a slow beat.

When it comes to Sun the lyrics go like this " Sun is not fit for sojourn....", the music notes gets tough where it becomes almost impossible for singing symbolizing the fact that sun is not a place to go near.

Both the man and the woman (the duet pair) after successfully completing their space sojourn reaches God alive who is Aanandaswaroopi. Indicative of this, the music is played by an electric guitar in basic Shruthi Utchasthayi (high pitched).

The song closes with resonating sound of the electric guitar.

Notes:

1. **From PBS' book "White Shadows"**
2. **From Mrs. P. Senthamilselvi's book "Innisai Chakravarthi: P.B. Srinivas"**
3. **Ibid**
4. **From Mrs. P. Senthamilselvi's book "Innisai Chakravarthi: P.B. Srinivas"**

CHAPTER 7

SONOROUS GHAZALS

A Ghazal is an elegant poetic innovation. Though the word 'Ghazal' has multiple meanings, it roughly means 'love talk with one's sweetheart'. Love, mutual attraction, affection and the related emotions and feelings are the basis for the creation of Ghazals.

P.B. Srinivos was by nature and nurture a poet. Being a polyglot, he was attracted toward Urdu language and literature in general and the genre Ghazal in particular. He wrote a number of Ghazals in Urdu, Hindi, Telugu, Tamil, Kannada and other languages, and recorded some of them apart from singing them in All India Radio from time to time.

Ghazal is a literary format developed in Persia in the 10th century. It is an elegant poetic innovation. Usually, it contains five to nine rhyming couplets. Ghazal as such is a lyric-poem. Hence, it contains both Arooz (prosody/rhyme) like a poem, and Bahar (rhythm) like a song.

Structure of a Ghazal (according to Quide-e-ghazal-e-Farsi): Each couplet is called a 'Sher'. The first Sher is called 'Matla' and the last Sher is called 'Makhta'.

Both the lines of Matla are rhyming lines and should contain rhyme words with a common identical terminal ending and an end sub rhyme. These are called Radeef and Qafia. Alternatively, the terms 'Hum Shakal' for Radeef and 'Hum Avaat' for Qafia can be used.

In all the other Shers, their second lines are the rhyming lines and hence should contain Radeef and Qafiya.

In some Ghazals, there may be one or more sub-rhymes in between Radeef and Qafiya, in which case the same sub-rhymes should be repeated in all the rhyming lines of that Ghazal.

The last Sher should contain the pen name of the poet, called 'Takhallus'. Most poets do give their pen names, but some don't. PBS' takhallus was 'Priya Bhashi' in his Telugu ghazals, and 'Shabaash' in his Urdu ghazals. He used to call his Telugu Ghazal as 'Vallari' which is a Telugu word.

The word ghazal roughly means 'love-talk with one's darling' - a dialogue between two beloveds (gufthagoo). Hence, it has been giving expression to such themes as love, appreciation of beauty, the ensuing separation, the resultant pain and sorrow. Love is the breath and life of the Ghazal writing. High intensity of imagination (khayal), ability to group words (lafzon ki bandish) cleverly and ideally, are needed to bring out a beautiful Ghazal.

Ghazaliyath (qualities of a Ghazal): Ghazal poets consider it as a feminine form. Hence, words like Ghazal ki nazakath (tenderness), Adaa (beauty), chaal-chalan (movement)etc. are often used and the same qualities are Incorporated in the Ghazal along with the expression of love, appreciation of beauty, separation and pain.[1]

With the above knowledge about Ghazals, let us read, understand and enjoy a few Ghazals of PBS[2]:

His Telugu ghazals
వల్లరి. No.1
* ప్రణయరాజ్యమునేలుప్రేయసి, రావేనాహృదయేశ్వరీ,
రసమయాధరసుధాకలశము, తేవేనాహృదయేశ్వరీ.
* ప్రేమరాగమునేనుపాడగమైమరచివినుచుందువు,
ప్రేమికునిననువీడి, ఇకపోలేవేనాహృదయేశ్వరీ.
* చెదుకోనీనవ్వుపువ్వులలోనితేనెలసారము,
నీదుసొబగులవెలుగులన్నియునావేనాహృదయేశ్వరీ.

* హాయిగానిదురించినాయెదకలచిమురియుచునుంటివి,
రాయికాదీమృదులహృదయము, పూవేనాహృదయేశ్వరీ.
* పలికెదనునీగుండెసవ్వడిలోననేప్రియభాషినై,
పలుకుమర్మముతెలియజాలకపోవేనాహృదయేశ్వరీ.
****

* Pranayarajyamu nelu preyasi, raave naa hrudayeswari,
Rasamayadhara sudhakalasamu, teve naa hrudayeswari.
* Premaraagamu nenu pandaga maimarachi vinuchunduvu,
Premikuni nanu veedi ika poleve naa hrudayeswari.
* Chedukonee, navvupuvvulaloni tenela saaramu,
Needu sobagula velugulanniyu, naave naa hrudayeswari.
* Haayigaa nidurinchi naa yeda kalachi muriyuchununtivi,
Raayikaadee mrudulahrudayamu, poove naa hrudayeswari.
Paluku marmamu teliyajaalaka pove naa hrudayeswari.
***

In the above Ghazal, the rhyming words (Qafia) are: Raave,teve, poleve, pove, naave, poove, with an identical terminal ending ‘ve'.The end rhyme (Qafia) is Hrudayeswari.

వల్లరి No:2
* నాచీకటిబ్రతుకులోనిదీపావళినీవేనే,
నవ్వులజల్లులుకురిసేతారావళినీవేనే.
* నాకంఠంనీవులేకవెలవెలబోయేను
నాగళానరత్నకుసుమహారావళినీవేనే.
* వెనవేలసుగుణాలనుమనసారామెచ్చుతూ,
నేనుసదాజపిస్తూన్ననామావళినీవేనే.
* నాకవితలుఅనుభవాలతొలిప్రతిబింబాలు,
నాజీవననవరసార్ధగాథావళినీవేనే.
* అందరితోకలిసిమెలిసితిరిగేప్రియభాషిని,
అహర్నిశలునేపాడేరాగావళినీవేనే.
***

* Naa cheekati bratukuloni deepaavali Neevene,
Navvula jallulu kurise taaraavali neevene.
* Naa khantam neevu leka vela vela boyenu,
Naa galana ratnakusuma haaraavali neevene.
* Venavela sugunaalanu manasaaraa mechhutu,

Nenu sadaa japistunna naamaavali neevene.
* Naa kavitalu anubhavaala toli pratibimbaalu,
Naa jeevana navarasaardra gaadhaavali neevene.
* Andarito kalisimelisi tirige Preyabhashini,
Aharniselu ne pade raagaavali neevene.
***

In the above Ghazal the rhyming words (Qafia) are: Deepaavali, taaraavali, haaraavali, naamaavali, gaadhaavali, raagaavali, withan identical terminal ending ‘aavali'.The end rhyme(Radeef) is Neevene.

****

వల్లరి No.3
* మనహృదయంమనకోవెల,
మనప్రణయంమనవెన్నెల.
* ప్రతినిమిషంనవభావన,
విరియునునీకనుసన్నల.
* రసఝరివలెమకరందము
కురియునునీతెలినవ్వుల.
* వలపులమామిడితోటలు,
కలవుచెలీనదికావల.
* ప్రియసఖినీప్రియభాషిని,
కొనిచనుమానీత్రోవల.
****

* Mana hrudayam mana kovela,
Mana pranayam mana vennela.
* Prati nimusham nava bhavana,
Viriyunu nee kanusannala.
* Rasajharivale makarandamu,
Kuriyunu nee telinavvula.
* Valapula mamiditotalu,
Kalavu cheli nadi kaavala.
* Priyasakhi nee priyabhashini,
Koni chanumaa nee Trovala.
***

In the above Ghazal the rhyming words (Qafia) are:

Kovela, Vennela, kanusannala, Navvula, Kaavala and Trovala with an identical terminal ending 'la'. In this Ghazal, these rhyming words are placed at the end of the rhyming lines. There is no separate End Rhyme(Radeef) as such.
Such Ghazal is called 'Anthyaprasa Ghazal' in Telugu and 'Gairmuraddaf ghazal' (Ghazal without Radeef) in Urdu by some poets.
* His Urdu Ghazals
He was supposed to have written over 400 ghazals in Urdu, out of which we could procure nearly 200 ghazals only. I am surprised to see that the intensity of his imagination is very high in Urdu and his command on the language is appreciable. His standard of writing is comparable to that of famous Urdu poets of the present day like Qateel Shifayee.
A few examples of PBS' excellent Urdu Ghazals:
* ग़ज़ल * No.1
* निगाहोंमेंपुरहैशरारतकाजादू।
तोबातोंमेंपुरहैलताफतकाजादू।।
* अदाओंमेंपुरहैनज़ाकतकाजादू।
इशारोंमेंपुरहैनफ़ासतकाजादू।।
* तेरीसादगीहैबहुतखूबसूरत।
बयानोंमेंपुरहैबलाग़तकाजादू।।
* तेरेहुस्नकाअक्सजोहैखुदाई।
नज़ारोंमेंपुरहैइबादतकाजादू।।
* वफ़ादार 'शाबाश' कीहैमोहब्बत।
गिलाओंमेंपुरहैशराफ़तकाजादू।।
***
* Nigahon mein pur hai, shararat ka jadu l
Toh baaton mein pur hai, latafat ka jadu l
* Adaon mein pur hai, nazakat ka jadu l
Isharon mein pur hai nafasat ka jadu l
*Teri sadgi hai bahut khubsurat l
Bayanon mein pur hai balaghat ka jadu ll
Tere husn ka aks jo hai khudai l
Nazaron mein pur hai ibaadat ka jadu ll
* Vafadar 'Shaabaash' ki hai mohabbat l

Gilaon mein pur hai sharafat ka jadu ll
***

The rhyming words in the above ghazal are:
Shararat, latafat, nazakat, nafasat, balagat,
Ibaadat, sharafat. The end rhyme is Jadu.
In this ghazal the second Sher is also a Matla.
This is called Husn-e-Matla.
****

- * ग़ज़ल* No.2
*आजचोटीपरचढ़ीहैआपकीशुहरतसनम।
रंगअपनाखोचुकीहैअबमेरीउल्फ़तसनम।।
*यहमेरीबेरंगउल्फ़तबेसहाराबनगई।
किसतरहहासिलकरेखोईहुईरंगतसनम।।
*आपकेहीदमसेपाईज़िन्दगीनेअहमियत।
मेरीहस्तीकीनहींहैअबकोईइज़्ज़तसनम।।
*शिद्दतेहसरतबढ़ीहैराहतेदीदारकी।
आपकारुख़देखकरजोहोगईमुद्दतसनम।।
*आपहैशक्लेवफ़ाशाबाशहैजिसपरफ़िदा।
आपपरउँगलीउठाएकिसकीहोजुरअतसनम।।
***

*Aaj choti par chadhi hai aap ki shuhurat sanam l
Rang apna kho chuki hai ab meri ulfat sanam ll
*Yeh meri berang ulfat be sahara bangayi l
Kis tarah hasil kare khoyi huyi rangat sanam ll
*Aap ke hi dam se paayi zindagi ne ahmiyat l
Meri hasti ki nahin hai ab koi izzat sanam ll
*Shiddate hasrat badhi hai rahate deedaar ki l
Aap kaa rukh dekh kar jo hogayi muddat sanam ll
*Aap hai shakle vafa 'Shaabaash' hai jis par fida l
Aap par ungli uthaye kis ki ho jurrat sanam ll
***

In the above Ghazal the rhyming words(Qafia) are:
Shuhrat, ulfat, rangat, izzat, muddat and jurrat,
ending with an identical terminal ending- at.
The end rhyme(Radeef) is Sanam.

******

* ग़ज़ल * No.3
* मुझेयूँभुलानामुबारकहोतुमको।
नज़रयूँचुरानामुबारकहोतुमको।।
* नलिखकरकोईख़त, ख़बरकुछनदेकर।
मेरादिलदुखानामुबारकहोतुमको।।
* तुम्हारीहीयादोंमेंतड़पूंमैंहरपल।
यहदूरीबढ़ानामुबारकहोतुमको।।
* फ़लकपरचढ़ाकरजमींपरबिठाया।
उठाकरगिरानामुबारकहोतुमको।।
* सदादीहै 'शाबाश' नेरूहोदिलसे।
नवादानिभानामुबारकहोतुमको।।
***
* Mujhe yun bhulaana mubarak ho tum ko l
Nazar yun churana mubarak ho tum ko ll
* Na likh kar koi khat, khabar kuch na de kar l
Mera dil dukhana mubarak ho tum ko ll
* Tumhari hi yadon mein tadapun mai har pal l
Yeh duri badhana mubarak ho tum ko ll
* Falak par chadhakar zamin par bithaya l
Utha kar girana mubarak ho tum ko ll
* Sada di hai 'Shaabaash' ne ruho dil se l
Na vaadaa nibhaana mubarak ho tum ko ll
***
In this Ghazal the rhyming words(Qafia) are: Bhulana, churana, dukhana, badhana, girana, nibhana.
The end rhyme(Radeef) is Tum ko.
Note: This ghazal is written in Persian style
With sub-rhymes between Radeef and Qafia.
They are mubarak and ho.
******

ग़ज़ल No.4
* मैंपैदाहुआहैतोतेरेलिए।
मैंज़िन्दारहाहूँतोतेरेलिए।।
* बनाक्यामैंअपनीहीख़ातिरसनम।

दिवानाबनाहूँतोतेरेलिए।।
* हसींमुझसेबेरुख़हैतेरीतरह।
मैंहँसनेलगाहूँतोतेरेलिए।।
* वफ़ाबेवफ़ाहोतोकुछराज़हो।
अगरबेवफ़ाहूँतोतेरेलिए।।
* मैंखाकरकरूँगाक़समपरक़सम।
जहाँसेख़फ़ाहूँतोतेरेलिए।।
***
* Mai paida huaa hai toh tere liye l
Mai zinda rahaa hun toh tere liye ll
* Bana kya mai apni hi khatir sanam l
Deewana banaa hun toh tere liye ll
* Hasin mujh se berukh hai teri tarah l
Mai hasne lagaa hun toh tere liye ll
* Wafa bewafa ho toh kuch raaz ho l
Agar bewafaa hun toh tere liye ll
* Mai kha kar kahunga khasam par khasam l
Jahan se khafaa hai toh 'Shaabaash' tere liye ll
***
In the above Ghazal the rhyming words (Qafia) are: huaa, rahaa,
Banaa, lagaa, bewafaa, khafaa. End rhyme(Radeef) is tere liye.
******
*ग़ज़ल * No.5
* हालातबदलतेजातेहैं।
जज़्बातबदलतेजातेहैं।।
* दिलपरजोलगेंआशिक़को।
सदमातबदलतेजातेहैं।।
* गातीहोजबवफ़ाभीबेसुर।
नगमातबदलतेजातेहैं।
* गमऔरखुशीकेदौरोंके।
लमहातबदलतेजातेहैं।।
* ज़ालिमहैंहसीनाकेजलावें।
दिनरातबदलतेजातेहैं।।

* मंज़िलभीबदलनेलगतीहै।
जब 'साथ' बदलतेजातेहैं।।
* 'शाबाश' कीमस्तीकेधुनमें।
सुरसातबदलतेजातेहैं।।
***
* Halaath badalte jaate hain l
Jazbaath badalte jaate hain ll
* Dil par jo lage aashik ko l
Sadmaath badalte jaate hain ll
* gaatee ho vafaa bhi jab be sur l
Nagmaath badalte jaate hain ll
* Gam aur khushi ke douron ke l
Lamhaath badalte jaate hain ll
* zaalim hai hasinaa ke jalve l
Din raat badalte jaate hain ll
* Manzil bhi badalne lagti hai l
Jab 'saath' badalte jaate hain ll
* 'Shabaash' ki masti ki dhun mein l
Sur saat badalte jaate hain ll
***
The rhyming words of the above Ghazal (Qafia) are:
Haalaath, jazbaath, sadmaath, nagmaath,
Lamhaath, din raath, jab saath and sur saath
with an identical terminal ending 'aath'.
All the rhyming lines of this Ghazal
Start with these rhyming words.
The Sub rhyming words are badalte and jaate.
The end rhyme (Radeef) is ‘hain’.

The Approach of PBS[3]:

Ghazal by itself demands a lot of attention whether it be in the form of poetry or by the way of rendition. PBS was very particular in pointing its features and gathering the subtleties and intricacies of the various styles of Ghazal. Having mastered Urdu poetry, he shared his opinion that ‘Reading the Ghazal' is the foremost thing that any singer should adhere to and begin with. It is the threshold to the journey of this complex form of Music- poetically and musically. As a poet, he meticulously followed the unceasing rhyming phrases and poetic expressions required for an ideal Ghazal under the pen name or 'Takhallus' - Shabash, and won acclaim for his literary work world wide.

If playback singing were his metier, Ghazal was his forte.PBS was a great admirer of Shahanshah-e-Ghazal, Mehdi Hassan and was inspired and influenced by Mehdi Hassan's extraordinary style of Ghazal rendition.

PBS' ghazals have the essence the authentic rendering on 'Sam of Taal'(pronounced as Sam) which denotes the point of rhythmic resolution.The 'Shadaj' or 'shadjamam' in Carnatic music is very eloquently placed in most of Mehdi Hassan's ghazals which makes his style unique and noteworthy. PBS adopted this style in many of his compositions adding the flavour and fragrance of the ghazal to the permutations and combinations of various 'swaras'.

Ghazal 'Adayagi' (presentation) and the accent were the most important aspects of Ghazal rendition to PBS. His staunch belief in 'Infaradujat' (individuality) of one's work made him a supremo. Although he was a great fan of Mehdi Hassan and Gulam Ali, the great Ghazal maestros, PBS had a distinct style of rendering ghazals which showed his originality both in presentations and compositions.

It should be mentioned that in 1963, a famous Telugu poet, Dasaradhi, wrote the first ghazal in Telugu, "Rammante chaalukaani rajyaalu vidichi raana/ Nee chinni Navvu kosam swargaalu gadachi raana." Another Telugu ghazal by Dasaradhi goes, "Adharaala veedhilona madhu shaalalunna daana" was sung by P.B. Srinivos in 1967 and the music was composed by Emani Shankara Shastri.Another ghazal which was written in Telugu by PBS and sung by him was "Kalpanalu sannayi oode vela chintalu denike" and was broadcast through All India Radio,Kadapa in 1978[4].

Thus, PBS' multi-talents were reflected in a number of genres including Ghazal writing and Ghazal singing.

Notes:

1. Aman Hindustani gave me this information.

2.I got the ghazals -Urdu and Telugu-from PBS' writings.

3. Devi Ramana Murthy gave me this analysis

4. I got this information from Rochismon's article.

غزل "بستمگر" (53)

تو نہیں جان سکے، زخم دل کی گہرائی!
روح نے رو کے بھی رخ پر ہنسی جو ٹھہرائی ॥

میری ہر شوخ نظر سب کو لگے ہرجائی!
دھڑکنوں نے تو ہمیشہ وفا کی دھن گائی ॥

یہ خزاں یوں ہے بستمگر، غم ہی غم دیکر
ہر بہار آئی مگر ساتھ خوشی کب لائی ॥

مل کے بھی مل نہ سکے، پیاس ہی بڑھی بے حد
اس سے بہتر تھی جدائی جو وقت نے ڈھائی ॥

آج شاباش پھرے بے پناہ و بے منزل
آنکھ نے دی جو تسلی تو دل نے ٹھکرائی ॥

Ghazal in Urdu

"نورِ جہاں!" (49)

اردو کے سب ہیں عاشق نورِ جہاں ہے اردو!
آبِ بقا سے بڑھ کر شیریں زباں ہے اردو ۔

جذبات تجربوں کے ہر موڑ پر نئے ہوں!
مشکل خیال کا بھی آساں بیاں ہے اردو ۔

اردو پہ حملہ ور ہوں گے بے شمار دشمن!
پائیگی ان پہ غلبہ جوشِ جواں ہے اردو ۔

آواز جسکی "شنکر" پتھر سی شے بھی پگھلے!
ہر غمزدہ کے دل کی جلتی فغاں ہے اردو ۔

ہر بات میں ترقی اردو نے کر لی حاصل!
رنگین جدّتوں کا زرّیں مکاں ہے اردو ۔

جس کے بدن پہ ہر دم علم و ادب کے تارے
رہتے ہیں جگمگاتے وہ آسماں ہے اردو ۔

شاباشؔ کی نظر میں بے حد ہے اس کی عزّت!
ہر شے کی روح کا جو عکسِ عیاں ہے اردو ۔

غزل نگار — ڈا. پی. بی. سرینواس
عرف — شاباشؔ آفتابِ کونا ڈی

Ghzal in Urdu

ಕಲ್ಪನೆಯ ಹಾರಾಟ ! "ಕನ್ನಡ ಘಜಲ್ (ಪಲ್ಲವಿ)"

ಕಲ್ಪನೆಯ ಹಾರಾಟ ಸಾಗುವ ವೇಳೆಯಲಿ, ವ್ಯರ್ಥ ವಿತರ್ಕೆ?
ಕವಿತೆಗಳ ಉಡುಗೊರೆಗಳ ಪೀಠವು, ತಾಯಿ ವಾಣಿಯ ಪಾದಕೆ॥

ಆತ್ಮಶಕ್ತಿಗೆ ಇಲ್ಲ ಅಪಜಯ, ವಿಜಯವೇ ಅದಕೆಂದಿಗೂ!
ಅಣುವಿನಲಿ ಬ್ರಹ್ಮಾಂಡ ತಿಳಿವುದು, ಆತ್ಮಶಕ್ತಿಯ ನೋಟಕೆ॥

ಹೂವನವು ತಾನಲ್ಲ ಜೀವನ, ಆಸೆಗಳ ನವರಾಂಗಣ!
ಯಾವ ಜೀವನದಲ್ಲಿ ದೊರೆಯಿತು? ಶಾಂತಿ ಬಯಕೆಯ ಕೋಟಕೆ॥

ನೆರಳಿನಂತೆಯೆ ಹಿಂದೆ ಬರುತಿಹ "ಭೀತಿ" ಭೂತವು, ನಿಜದಲಿ!
ನಿನಗೆ ಮರಳಾಪದೊಮ್ಮೆ ತಾನೇ, ಬಿಡುಗಡೆಯ ಕೊಡು ಭೂತಕೆ॥

ಸೃಷ್ಟಿಯಲಿ ಬಹುವರ್ಣ ದೀಪಗಳುಂಟು, ಕತ್ತಲ ನೀಗಲು;
ಕ್ಷೇಮಕರ, ಬೆಳಕಲ್ಲಿ ಪಯಣವ ನಡೆಸುತಿರೋಣ ಲೋಕಕೆ॥

ಗೀತೆಗಳ ರಸಪೂರ್ಣ ಧಾಟಿಗೆ, ಪ್ರಾಣವಲ್ಲವೆ? ಪಲ್ಲವಿ!
ಪಲ್ಲವಿಯು ತಾನಿಲ್ಲದಿದ್ದರೆ, ಗಮನವಲ್ಲದೆ? ಚರಣಕೆ॥

Ghazal in Kannada

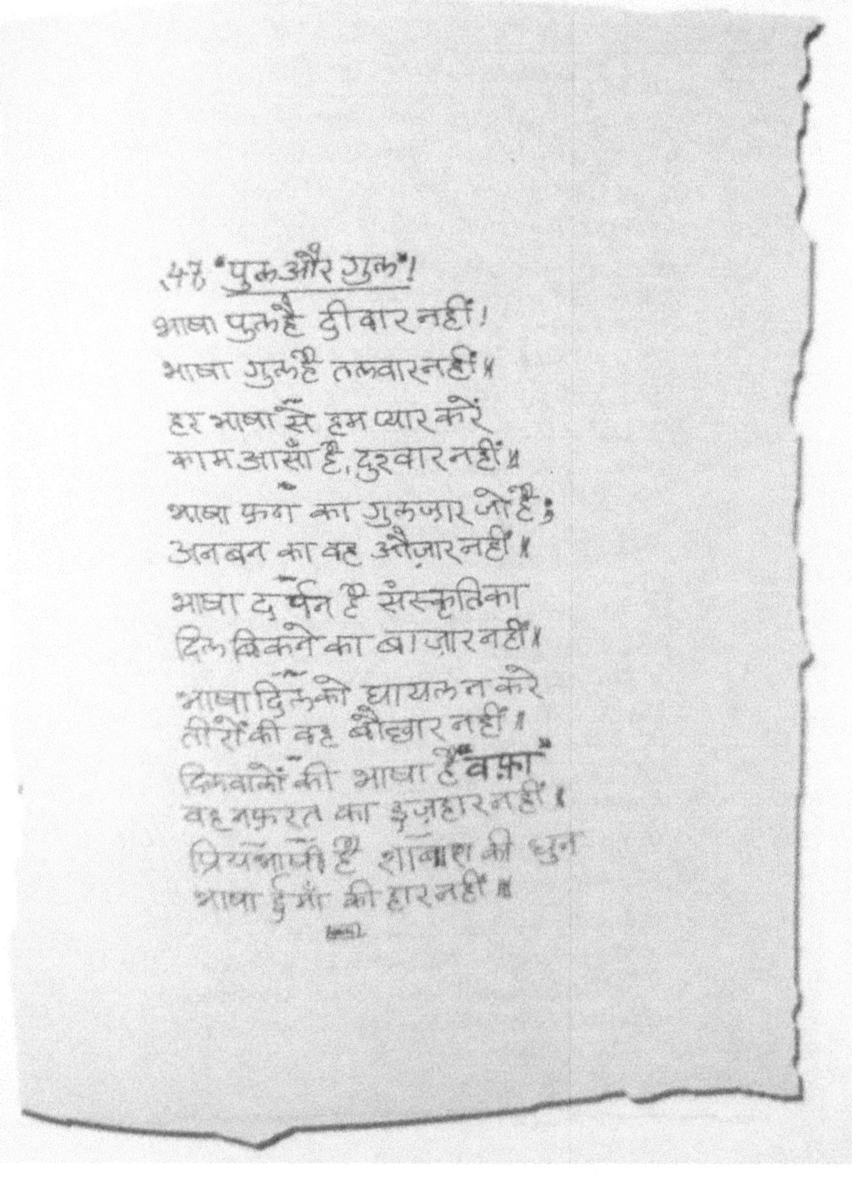

47 "पुल और गुल"!
भाषा पुल है दीवार नहीं।
भाषा गुल है तलवार नहीं॥
हर भाषा से हम प्यार करें
काम आसाँ है, दुश्वार नहीं॥
भाषा फ़न का गुलज़ार जो है;
अनबन का वह औज़ार नहीं॥
भाषा दर्पन है संस्कृति का
दिल बिकने का बाज़ार नहीं॥
भाषा दिल को घायल न करे
तीरों की वह बौछार नहीं॥
दिलवालों की भाषा है "वफ़ा"
वह नफ़रत का इज़हार नहीं॥
प्रियभाषी है शांति की धुन
भाषा दुश्मों की हार नहीं॥

Ghazal in Hindi

(41) "The Essence (Lake) of Poetry!"

Hindi is an enlightening Language!
It is the ambition of Progress and prosperity!!
Hindi is the Gem-Garland of Virtues!
It is the Tavern of melody and Sweetness!!
Hindi renders Service to all!
The entire world is enraptured by Hindi!
Let Every-one love Hindi!
Hindi is the Essence (Lake) of Poetry!!
There is Music filled in Hindi!
Hindi is the Symbol of friendship!
Hindi is the Mode of Culture!
Hindi does win victory always!!
Hindi joins hearts with hearts!
It makes flowers blossom in the Mind-Garden!!
Hindi awakens sleeping souls!
It Sings the praise of the Greatness of God!!
Hindi is the form of the Sculpture of imagination!
It comforts all, like Sunshine in winter!!
Hindi is the torch-Light of Hope!
It is the Principle (code) Equality!!
Let us all learn Hindi, with Love & affection!
Let us see every-thing, through the View-finder of Hindi!
Good-Knowledge can be obtained by the help of Hindi!
The Nation can get progress, through Hindi!!
Hindi Brings New illuminations!
Let us always be the Patrons of Hindi!
May the Indian Woman (Hindi) be victorious!
May the Hindi-Language always Succeed!!!

Ghazal in English

41 "कविता का सार।"

हिन्दी सुरुचिर भाषा है।
अभ्युदय की अभिलाषा है॥
सद्गुणों की मणिमाला है।
मधुरिमा की मधुशाला है॥

सब की सेवा करती है।
दुनिया इस पर मरती है॥
हिन्दी से हो सब को प्यार!
हिन्दी है कविता का सार॥

भरा है हिन्दी में संगीत!
हिन्दी है स्नेह का संकेत॥
संस्कृति की हिन्दी है रीत!
हिन्दी की सदा होगी जीत॥

हिन्दी दिल से दिल को मिलाये!
मन के चमन में फूल खिलाये॥
सोयी आत्माओं को जगाये!
प्रभु की महिमा गाके सुनाये॥

कल्पना-शिल्प का है रूप!
जाड़े में हिन्दी है धूप॥
हिन्दी है आशा की ज्योति!
हिन्दी है समता की नीति॥

प्रेम से हम सब हिन्दी सीखें।
हिन्दी की नज़र से, सब देखें॥
हिन्दी से मिले, सब को सन्मति!
हिन्दी से मिले, देश को प्रगति॥
हिन्दी लाये नये उजियाले।
हिन्दी के बनें हम रखवाले॥
जय हो भारत भाषा की!
जय हो हिन्दी भाषा की॥

Ghazal in Hindi

(53) "Afflictor"! "Ghazal"

You can never know the depth of the wound
of my heart!
Because my soul, though weeping internally,
has planted a Smile on my face, externally!!
—
Each of my mischievous looks, looks (appears)
a vagabond to everybody!
But my heart-beats sing always only the
Song (tune) of faith!!
—
The autumn is continuing its atrocity,
giving me Sorrow and Sorrow alone!
When did any of the Springs that have come,
brought any joy along with it??
—
We've met but yet couldn't meet and
thirst alone has grown very much!
I think, the seperation imposed on us,
was much better!!
—
To-day, Shaalbaash is wandering without
any Shelter or goal!
My heart has refused the Consolation
offered by the eye!!!

Ghazal in English

CHAPTER 8

MELODIOUS MEDLEY

I

PBS, being a polyglot, not only sang film songs but also rendered a number of the traditional Stotras, Dandakams and Ashtakams in Sanskrit. It is a well-known fact that Ghantasala was a pioneer in the renditions of the Stotras, Dandakams and Ashtakams. His 'Bani' (style of rendition) was followed by many singers in the Southern India. PBS, in stead of following his senor Ghantasala's 'Bani', created his own 'Bani' which reflects in the following:

- Sri Raghavendra Suprabhata
- Sri Virupaksha Suprabhata
- Sri Srinivas Suprabhata
- Sri Lakshmi Narasimha Suprabhata
- Sri Krishnashtakam
- Sri Pandurangashtakam
- Sri Ramamangalashtakam
- Sri Venkatesa Stotram
- Sri Hayagriva Stotram
- Sri Ranganatha Stotram
- Sri Lakshmi Narasimha Karavalamba Stotram
- Navagraha Storam
- Sri Lakshmi Stotram
- Sri Sharada Bhujanga Stotram

- Mukundamala
- Shiva Tandavam
- Hanuman Chalisa

PBS' renditions were appreciated by Sri Periyavar Chandrasekhareswara Swami, Sri Tridandi Chinna Srimannarayana Ramanuja Jeer Swami, and Swami Sukhabodhananda. By rendering Mukundamala of Sri Kulasekhara Alwar, PBS did yeoman service to the Vishnu Bhaktas in general and Sri Vaishanavite community in particular[1].

II

PBS, as a budding singer, for the first time sang in a Hindi movie titled "Mr. Sampath" which was based on a novel with the same title written by R.K. Narayan. Though PBS was from Andhra, his pronunciation of Hindi was impeccable. The songs 'Aaj Hum Bharat Ki Naari' and 'Chalo Pania Bharan ko' gave importance to female voices, but the point to be noted was that he sang in the company of Shamshad Begum, Geeta Roy (who later married the famous thespian Guru Dutt) Talat Mehmood and Jikki. PBS sang a few lines individually and the rest he sang in chorus. PBS started singing for dubbed movies too.[2]

For the Hindi movie "Mai Bhi Ladki Hun", its music composer Chitra Gupt wanted singers of the stature of Mohd Rafi of the Hindi field to sing a duet with Lata Mangeshkar.As he could not get them, the final offer went to P.B Srinivos of the South. As PBS puts it, "*Daane daane par likha hai khane wale ka naam/ gaane gaane par likha hai gaane vale ka naam*"[3]. PBS sang the duet 'Chanda Se Hoga Jo Pyara' with Lata Mangeshkar, the Nightingale of India. Needless to say that PBS venerated the great singer.

PBS not only sang songs in Hindi, but also wrote songs in Hindi, Tamil, Telugu, and Kannada which were sung by S. Janaki and S.P. Balu in different movies. For the Telugu movie "Aakali Rajyam", he wrote the song 'Tuhi Raja Tuhi Rani'. For the movie "Manchi Roju", he wrote the song 'Cheppalanundi Cheppedela'.

In Kannada movies too, he wrote Hindi songs wherever Hindi songs was necessary.

III

P.B. Srinivos sung in at least 13 Tulu movies, said Tamma Laxmana, an art director associated with Tulu cinemas. The popular Tulu song 'Daane ponne' from Bolli Thota was sung by him.

Mr. Laxmana said that the first Tulu cinema to hit the screens was Enna Tangadi. Srinivas did not sing in it. The second cinema was Dareda Budedi, in which PBS sang 'Nikkade dumbiyad barpe'. Thereafter, he sang in many Tulu cinemas.

He had sung 'anyayano vichitrano' in Bisatti Babu, 'jodu nanda deepa' written by Amrut Someshwar Koti Chennayya. PBS also sang in Dareda Seere, Bhagyavantedi, Saviradorthi Savithri, Aer Maltina Tappu, Bayya Mallige, Kasdaye Kandane, Yan Sanyasi Ape, Udalda Tudar and Pageta Puge.[4]

IV

PBS sang in Konkani too which became popular - the popular song is 'Mog Tuzo Kitlo Ashlon'.[5]

Notes:

1.Taken from the book P. Senthaminselvi's 'Innisaichakravarthi: P.B.Srinivos'

2. Ibid

3. PBS' oft quoted words

4. Taken from The Hindu,15 April, 2013.

5. We should note that the mother tongue of Lata Mangeshkar and Asha Bhonsle is Konkani.

With Asha Bhonsle

With Lata Mangeshka

CHAPTER 9
POLYGLOT AND BARD FROM THE GODAVARI

"*Vaagaardhaviva Sampruktau*

Vagardha Pratipattaye

Jagatah Pitarau vande

Parvati Parameswarau"

-Mahakavi Kalidasa[1]

I

To recapitulate, we have analysed in the first chapter the amount of enthusiasm and penchant on the part of PBS for acquiring a command over languages. Throughout his life, PBS maintained the same amount of enthusiasm and fascination for languages and literatures, and acquired an enviable command over 8 languages, namely Sanskrit, Telugu, Tamil, Kannada, Malayalam, English, Hindi and Urdu. He used to speak, write and sing in eight languages.Generally speaking, a number of playback singers sang and are singing in languages other than their respective languages by noting it down in the script of their respective mother tongues, but not in the script of the language in which they would sing the song. But PBS was unique in noting down the lyrics of the song, say in Malayalam, in the script of Malayalam itself, but not in the script of his mother tongue, Telugu.

PBS was a prolific writer. He wrote poems and prose, short stories and short(one-act) plays. He wrote ghazals in Urdu and Hindi, Tamil and Kannada.

like me who was trained in research skills, it appears as though PBS was a trained researcher: his prose in Telugu is precise and incisive, replete with a sense of humor and marvellous felicity of expression.

After shifting to Madras, PBS was associated with scholars like Bulusu VenkataRamaniah, Theertham Sridhara Murty and V. Raghavan; also, his literary activity increased due to his close association with Devulapalli Krishna Shastri, Malladi Ramakrishna Shastri, Srisri, Anisetty Subba Rao, Cheruvu Anjaneya Shastri, and Kongara Jaggaiah. At the feet of Ravuri Doraswami Sharma, PBS learnt Telugu 'Chandassu' along with Arudra. In those days, the budding singer cum writer studied the complexities and subtleties of Telugu "Chandassu" with the guidance of Doraswami Sharma and with the help of a scholar like B. Nagaraja Rao, he made forays into Kannada "chandassu" also. (The knowledge acquired during this period must have stood him in good stead while conversing with scholars in Karnataka.) With the profundity acquired by PBS, he did research on Telugu "chandassu" and created new "Chandovruttams" like "Gayatri Vruttamu" and "Srinivasa Vruttamu".

The following were the creations of PBS the poet:

A. Gayatri Vruttam and Dasa Geeta Geeta Sandesam[3]

గాయత్రీవృత్తము

ఆఆలోచనేశ్రీనివాస్‌కితెలుగుఛందశ్శాస్త్రవిజ్ఞాతృ
మండలిలోఅజరామరమైనస్థానాన్నికల్పించింది.
'గాయత్రీవృత్తము'అనేఅపూర్వమైనప్రయోగాన్నిచే
శారు.
షడ్వింశతిచ్ఛందాలకుఒక్కొక్కదానికిఒక్కొక్కటిప్ర
తీకగా 26 గణాలనుతీసుకొన్నారు.
ఈప్రక్రియనుఇంకావిస్తరించటానికిఅవకాశంఉన్న

దని,
అందుకుగురుస్థానంతమదేననిసూచించటానికిఒక'గురువు'నుఆపైనినిలిపారు. మొత్తం 26 X 3 = 78 + 1 = 79
అక్షరాలతోభారతీయపద్యసాహిత్యచరిత్రలోఅపూర్వమైనగాయత్రీవృత్తమును 1979లోరచించారు.
1979లోరచించినందువల్ల 79
అక్షరాలుకూర్చారనుకొంటాను.
వాటినిఆయనపరిభాషలోచెప్పాలంటే—
ముందుగానాలుగేసిగణాలతోపదహారుఅక్షరాలచొప్పునఆఱుగణపతాకలనుకూర్చుకొన్నారు.
అవిఇరవైనాలుగుగణాలుఅయ్యాయి.
అక్కడికిడెబ్బైరెండుఅక్షరాలువచ్చాయి.
ఆపైనిరెండులఘువులను, ఒకగురువును,
మూడులఘువులను, ఒకగురువునునిలిపారు.
అవిఏడుఅక్షరాలు.
మొత్తానికిడెబ్బైతొమ్మిదిఅక్షరాలు.

ఆయనపేర్కొన్నగణాలక్రమప్రథఇది:

తసయమ; యజయమ; యజతమ; తసయమ; యజయమ; తరయమ; II U III U

ఈగురులఘువులఅనుక్రమణిఒకపాదానికిమాత్రం చూస్తేఈవిధంగాఉంటుంది:

UUI (త) IIU (స) IUU (య) UUU (మ);

IUU (య) IUI (జ) IUU (య) UUU (మ);

IUU (య) IUI (జ) UUI (త) UUU (మ);

UUI (త) IIU (స) IUU (య) UUU (మ);

IUU (య) IUI (జ) IUU (య) UUU (మ);

UUI (త) UIU (ర) IUU (య) UUU (మ);

II;

U;

III;

U.

ఇదిగణక్రమం. తసయమ;
యజయమఅన్నక్రమంరెండుపర్యాయాలురావటం వల్లపద్యపాదంశ్రుతిసుభగంగాఉన్నమాటనిజమేకా నిపాదంచివఅనుస-న-గఅనిగణాలనువ్యపదేశించక, లేదాలల-గ-లలల-గఅనిపేర్కొనక II U III U అనిగురులఘుసంకేతాలనునిర్దేశించటంవల్లశ్రీనివా స్ఏమివైచిత్రినిసాధింపదలిచారోతెలియదు. 'నాచిత్రరచనలునావిగాన'అనుకొన్నారేమో! లాక్షణికపద్ధతిఅనుసారంగణక్రమాన్నిఈవిధానడ దాహరించాలి:

తసయమ; యజయమ; యజతమ; తసయమ;
యజయమ; తరయమ; సనగ.

నిజానికివీటిలోత-స-య-
మగణాలది'అంభోజాలి'అన్నసమవృత్తమనిదుఃఖ
భంజనుడుతన *వాగ్వల్లభం*లోపేర్కొన్నాడు.
దీనికి *విశాలాంభోజాలి* అనికూడాపేరున్నది.
ఈవిధంగాప్రస్తరిస్తేఈగాయత్రీవృత్తమువివిధలఘు
చ్ఛందాలసమాహారవృత్తమవుతుంది.
పరిశోధకులకుఈవ్యాసంగంఒకక్రీడాక్షేత్రం.
పద్యపాదాలలోనియతిస్థానాన్నికూడాశ్రీనివాస్నిర్దే
శించారు. 79 అక్షరాలపాదంలో 1 – 13 – 25 – 37 –
49 – 61 యతిస్థానాలు.
మొదటిఅక్షరంకాకఐదుయతులన్నమాట.
వృత్తంకాబట్టిప్రాసనియతం.
దీనినితమతల్లిదండ్రులకుఅంకితంచేస్తూ'జననీజ
నకగాయత్రీవృత్తము'అనిసంజ్ఞానించారు.
తమశ్రీమత్తకు, నేతృత్వధాతృత్వాలకు,
క్షేమైశ్వర్యాలకుకారయిత్రికాబట్టితల్లిదండ్రులరూపు
గొన్నగాయత్రీదేవినిసన్నుతించారు.
'అపూర్వప్రాశస్త్యోద్ధృతి'మూలానఈవృత్తంప్రసిద్ధికి
నోచుకొనగలదనిఆకాంక్షించారు.
పరిమాణంలోచిన్నదేఅయినా,
కరపత్రగ్రంథరూపంలోశ్రీనివాస్వెలువరించినతొలి
పుస్తకంఇదే. 1979లోఅచ్చయింది.

గాయత్రీవృత్తముకరపత్రంలోనిపద్యంఇది:

మొదటిపాదం:

[శ్రీ]మంతుఁడనునేనుశ్రీగాయత్రీస[త్కృ]పన్,
దేవి పేరవినూత్న చ్ఛందంబుల్ [సృ]జింపంగ,
నేఁడునాచేతనౌటన్, నే[తృ]త్వంబొసంగి, దేవి,
నాకీరీతిన్ధా[తృ] శక్తిస్వరంబుగనిచ్చెన్శ్రీగాయ[త్రీ]
భవ్యభావ్యదివ్యమాహాత్మ్యంబున్,
వర్ణనసేయఁదరమే?

రెండవపాదం:

[క్షే]మార్థబహుమానితైశ్వర్యంబుల్పు[ష్టి]మీఱంగఁ
బొంది, సదాదాసులన్సంతు[ష్టిఁ] జేతమ్ముఁపొంగ,
వేనోళ్ళఁబాడంగా,
[శ్రే]యస్కరకృపార్ద్రదృష్టిన్సంరక్షిం[చి],
విశ్వంబునేలునహోరాత్రంబుల్, పో[షిం]పంగ,
జీవరాసులన్దానైసన్నద్ధయగున్వరదయై,

మూడవపాదం:

[భూ]మిన్నిజదయాసుధావృష్టిన్వేఁద[న్పు]చున్;
గానన్నాజననీధ్యానంబున్స[ల్పు]చున్పాదపద్మయు
గ్మంబుభావాలన్
[బూ]జింపుచునుభక్తినర్పింతుగ్రంథం[బు],
నాతల్లిశేషగిరమ్మనాన్సధ్వినన్[తు]ణ్యార్థసంయుతు
న్ఫణీంద్రస్వామిన్, నాజనకున్దలఁచుచున్,

నాలుగవపాదం:

[ధీ]మజ్జనఘనప్రశంసార్హాలై,
సి[ద్ధి]నందంగఁజాలునపూర్వప్రాశస్త్యో[ద్ధృ]తిన్సర్వ

భాగ్యముల్గొన్న శ్రీగాయ[త్రీ]
వృత్తములునాయశస్సామ్రాజ్యంబున్
[స్థి]రప్రాభవంబునఁబాలింపంగా,
వృ[ద్ధి]జెందుచుండి,
వారియాశీర్వాదంబుల్గొనుచున్మెఱయఁగన్.

ఈవిధంగాఅక్షరచ్ఛందస్సులపరిధినివిస్తరించినంతమాత్రానసరిపోదు.
అదికేవలంవైనోదికప్రక్రియామాత్రవిశేషంగాపర్యవసిస్తుంది.
పైగాగాయత్రీవృత్తములోచెప్పుకోదగిన‘గతి’అంటూఏమీలేదు.
అందువల్లశ్రీనివాస్ఈపరిధినిమఱింతగావిస్తరించి, 1979లోనే“సహనశక్తియును, కల్పనాప్రాభవంబును, భావాధిక్యతయు”కలిగినఅత్యంతాపూర్వమైన“శ్రీనివాసవృత్తము”నుప్రకల్పించారు.
వెనుకకరపత్రంగాముద్రించినగాయత్రీవృత్తముతోకలిపిదీనినిశ్రీనివాసశ్రీగాయత్రీవృత్తములుఅన్న పేరిటఒకలఘుపుస్తకంగాముద్రించారు.
తెలుగుఛందోరీతులలోఇదిఒకఅపూర్వమైనప్రకరణం.
అందుకునైపథ్యానుసంజనగాకొన్నినవీనవృత్తాలనుకల్పించారు.
ఆకల్పనకొక్కొండవేంకటరత్నం *విరచితబిల్వేశ్వరీయము*నుచూడటంవల్లతీగసాగింది.
ఆయనకల్పించినఆనవీనవృత్తాలివి:

- ర-స-మ-య-స-మ-య

- జ-ల-జ-న-య-న
- ర-మా-త-న-య
- న-త-జ-నా-వ-న
- న-గ-రా-జ-త-న-యా
- సా-గ-ర-త-న-యా

ఈవృత్తాలపేర్లన్నీఅందులోనిగణాలేకావటంవిశేషం
.
దీర్ఘంవచ్చినచోటఅదిరెండుగణాలనిగుర్తుంచుకోవాలి. రమాతనయఅంటేర-మ-మ-త-న-యగణాలన్నమాట. ఈక్రమప్రథతోశ్రీనివాస్-

ర-స-మ-య-రా-మ-నా-మ-భ-జ-న-ర-త-జ-న-తా-మా-న-స

అన్నగణాలతో 23 X 3 = 69
అక్షరాలఒకసమవృత్తాన్నిచిత్రంగాప్రకల్పించారు.
ఆపద్యానికి'రసమయరామనామభజనరతజనతామానస'అనిపేరుపెట్టారు.
ఈచిత్రంఇంతకుమునుపులాక్షణికులుచేసినదేఅయినా,
ఒకపద్యానికిఇంతపెద్దపేరునుపెట్టడంకూడావిశేషమే.
ఇంతసుదీర్ఘమైనవృత్తంఎన్నోఛందస్సులోఏన్నోవృత్తంఅన్నవిచికిత్సవిద్యార్థులకైనానిర్నిమిత్తమే అవుతుంది. ఇకపంచతాళవృత్తాలలోనూ,
శ్రీకళాస్తంభకల్పనవిషయంగానూశ్రీనివాస్చేసినపరి

శోధనసారాన్ని అన్యలాక్షణికులనిర్వచనాలతోసరి పోల్చితులనాత్మకంగావేఱొకవ్యాసంలోవివరించ టంబాగుంటుందనిపించిఇక్కడఆవివరణనుకూర్చ టంలేదు.
ఈకృషిసమస్తంశ్రీనివాస్సరిక్రొత్తగాపింగళుడు, కేదారభట్టుమొదలైనప్రాచీనులపంక్తిపావనధోరణి లో'శ్రీనివాసవృత్తము'అనేవృత్తసృష్టినిచేశారు.

శ్రీనివాసవృత్తము

శ్రీనివాసవృత్తములోపాదానికి 116 అక్షరాలుంటాయి. వాటిగణాలక్రమప్రథఇది:

UUU (మ) – IIU (స) – IUI (జ) – IIU (స) – UUI (త) – UUI (త) – UUU (మ) – UUI (త) – III (న) – IUU (య) – IUU (య) – IUU (య) – IIU (స) – UII (భ) – UIU (ర) – III (న) – UUU (మ) – IUU (య) – IUU (య) – IIU (స) – IUI (జ) – IIU (స) – IIU (స) – IIU (స) – IUI (జ) – UII (భ) – IIU (స) – IUI (జ) – IIU (స) – IIU (స) – IIU (స) – IUI (జ) – UIU (ర) – UUU (మ) – UII (భ) – III (న) – UUI (త) – UUI (త) – U (గ) – U (గ)

ఇవి 38 గణాలపైరెండుగురువులుఅన్నమాట. మొత్తం [38 X 3]+2 = 114 + 2 = 116 అక్షరాలు. పద్యోదాహరణంఇది:

మొదటిపాదం:

[శ్రీ] సప్తాచలవాస! శ్రీశ! వరదా! [శ్రీ] శ్రీనివాసా!
స్ఫుర[ద్ర్చీ]వక్షా! వేంకటరమణ! సం[సే]వితాంఘ్రీ!
మురారీ! [స్మి]తవక్త్రా! జితకోటిమన్మథ! హరీ!
[శ్రే]యస్కరా! శ్రీధరా! [జీ]వనభాగ్యదాత!
సర[సీ]రుహలోచన! లోకపావనా! [శ్రి]తజనపోష!
నిర్గుణ! వ[శీ]కృతభక్తజనౌఘమానసా!
[చి]దానందాత్మా! సర్వసుఖశుభదా!
[శే]షపర్యంకశాయీ!

తక్కిననాలుగుపాదాలూఈవిధంగానేఉంటాయి. 1 – 13 – 20 – 30 – 37 – 50 – 57 – 66 – 77 – 87 – 98 స్థానాలలోయతినిలుపబడింది.
వృత్తంకనుకప్రాసనియతిఉన్నది.

డైమండ్క్

ఇదేకాలంలోశ్రీనివాస్సంగీతమేళకర్తరాగాలస్వరలక్షణాన్ని,
రాగస్వరూపాన్నిగుర్తుంచుకోవటానికి'వైరఇసై'అనబడేఒక'డైమండ్క్'సూత్రాన్నిరూపొందించారు.
ఇదివారిరాగస్వరూపాభిజ్ఞతకు,
గణితశాస్త్రకోవిదత్వానికి,
స్వరగ్రామసంగ్రహాన్నివిద్యార్థులకునేర్పివారివిద్యార్థిత్వానికిప్రాతిపదికనుకూర్చాలనిచేసినప్రయత్నం.
ఇప్పటికేపెద్దదవుతున్నఈప్రస్తావికలోదీనివిపులవివరణనుఇవ్వటంలేదు.
శ్రీనివాస్దీనిని ప్రకటించినవెంటనేభారతరత్నఎం.ఎస్. సుబ్బులక్ష్మి, పద్మవిభూషణ్డి.కె. పట్టమ్మాళ్,

రతి–
దరధ్వనితాళముమొదలైనపద్యాలతోశ్రీవాణీపద్మాం బారతిదరధ్వనితాళముఅనేగర్భచిత్రాన్నిరూపొం దించి, అప్పకవీయంలోదానినినివేశింపజేశాడు.
గణపవరపువేంకటకవితన *ప్రబంధరాజవేంకటేశ్వర విజయవిలాసములో*
808వపద్యంగాఒకఅపూర్వమైనగర్భబంధచిత్రాన్ని ప్రకల్పించాడు.
నాదెండ్లపురుషోత్తమకవితమఅద్భుతోత్తరరామాయ ణములోఎన్నివేలవిధాలుగాఅయినాచదవటానికివీ లుండేఒకసీసపద్యాన్నివ్రాసినసంగతిఅందరికీతెలి సినదే.
అయితేఅవన్నీఒకప్రసిద్ధమైనపద్యంలోఎన్నోమఱి కొన్నిప్రసిద్ధమైనపద్యాలనుగర్భితంగాకూర్చేచిత్రర చనలు. సంస్కృతంలోనూ,
తెలుగులోనూఅటువంటివిపదులకొద్దీకావ్యాలున్నా యి. కానీశ్రీనివాప్రచనఅటువంటిదికాదు.
ఒకగాయత్రీవృత్తంలోనుంచి,
ఒకశ్రీనివాసవృత్తంలోనుంచిపాఠకుడుశ్రీకళాస్తంభ సూత్రాన్నిఅనుసరించి
(దీనినిమఱొకవ్యాసంలోవివరిస్తాననిఇందాకఅన్నా ను) తెలుగువృత్తము,
ఉమర్ఖయామ్వృత్తముమొదలైనకొత్తవృత్తాలనుతన ఇష్టానుసారంసృష్టించుకోవటానికివీలుంటుంది.
ఆవృత్తాలకుపాఠకుడుపెట్టుకోవలసినపేర్లసూత్రం గుర్తుంచేవందలకొద్దీపద్యాలనుగర్భితంగానిర్మింప వచ్చునన్నమాట.
ఆవిధంగాఇదిచిత్రకావ్యవాఙ్మయానికిఒకఅపూర్వమై నఅలంకారం.

“గాయత్రీవృత్తమునవ్యము, భవ్యము, స్తవ్యము. ఇదియరసిచూడగా, బహుశఃఆనాటివేంకటరత్నముఈనాటిశ్రీనివాస్‌గానవతరించెనేమోయనినాయనుమానము”అనిపీఠికనువ్రాసినశ్రీరావూరిదొరసామిశర్మఅన్నారు.

దశగీతగీతసందేశం

శ్రీనివాసగాయత్రీవృత్తరచనానంతరంశ్రీనివాస్రచించినమఱొకచిత్రకావ్యంఇది. పేరుకుదశగీతమేకాని, నిజానికిఇందులోమొత్తంపదకొండుగీతపద్యాలున్నాయి. గ్రంథముద్రణసంవత్సరంలేదుకాని, వెనుకఅట్టమీద 1978లోఅచ్చయిన‘లవ్లీలవ్సాంగ్స్’ఆంగ్లగీతాలసంపుటిముద్రణవిషయంఉన్నది. ఇదివీరితృతీయప్రకటనఅనిఉన్నది. 1980లోలవ్లీలవ్సాంగ్స్ద్వితీయముద్రణవెలువడింది. కనుక 1979 ఏప్రిల్నెలలలోశ్రీనివాసగాయత్రీవృత్తములుప్రకటించినవెంటనేదీనిప్రకాశనజరిగినదనిఊహించాలి. ఆంధ్రప్రదేశ్ఆస్థానకవిదాశరథి, విద్వాన్రావూరిదొరసామిశర్మ, ప్రముఖచలనచిత్రనిర్మాతఎం.ఎస్. రెడ్డిఅభిప్రాయాలనువ్రాశారు. శ్రీనివాస్ధర్మపత్ని“ఆత్మసఖియైననాదానికి”శ్రీమతిజానకికిఇదిఅంకితం.

దశగీతగీతసందేశంఒక‘అంతర్లాపి’వర్ణచిత్రకావ్యం. ఒకపద్యంలోగర్భితంగాకొన్నిఅక్షరాలుంటాయి.

ఆఅక్షరాలనుకలుపుకొనిచదివితేఒకలఘువాక్యంఅ
వుతుంది. అంటే,
ఒకవాక్యాన్నికవిముందుగాకూర్చుకొని,
దానిచుట్టూపద్యపాదాలనుఅల్లుతాడన్నమాట.
ఇదిచక్రబంధం, నాగబంధం,
రథబంధంమొదలైనబంధచిత్రాలలోనూఉన్నదే.
చ్యుతకచిత్రాలలోనూఇటువంటిఇటువంటిధోరణిఉ
న్నది.
సంస్కృతంలోమేఘవిజయగణి *దిగ్విజయమహాకా
వ్యం*లోనూ, లోలింబరాజు *వైద్యకరాజీయం* లోనూ;
తెలుగులోవావిలికొలనుసుబ్బారావు *కౌసల్యాపరిణ
యం*లోనూ,
అల్లమరాజురంగశాయికవి *చంపూభారతము* లోనూ
ఇటువంటి'అంతర్లాపి'చిత్రరచనలున్నాయి.
పద్యాలతోపాటుశ్రీనివాస్ఇందులోగేయాలనుకూడా
వ్రాశారు.
కావ్యంనుంచిపద్యాన్నిగాకఒకగేయాన్నిమాత్రంచూ
పుతాను:

నియ[మా]లన్నీపాటించాలి!
సమ[తా]గానముసాగించాలి!
భేద[పి]శాచమువిజృంభించితే!
కుల[త]త్త్వాలకుశిరసువంచితే!
చన[రు] జనులైకమత్యపుదారిని!
కాకు[లు] నవ్వునుచూసివారిని!
మన[దే]శానికిసంఘటనబలము!
మాన[వ] ప్రగతిమనఆదర్శము!
బాధ్య[త] అంతాసదాప్రజలదే!
కొల్ల[లు]గపండుపంటజనులదే!

ఇదిగేయం.
ఇందులోకవితాసౌందర్యానికంటేచిత్రకల్పనకేప్రా
ధాన్యండున్నా,
తక్కినచిత్రకవులవలెనేశ్రీనివాస్భావసౌందర్యానికి,
వ్యర్థపదాడంబరంలేనిసుందరభావచిత్రనిర్మితికి
ప్రాధాన్యంఇచ్చారు.
దశగీతగీతసందేశంలోనిపదిగీతాలలోఈవిధంగాశ్రీని
వాస్పిల్లలుతల్లిదండ్రులనుఏవిధంగాఆరాధించా
లోపదిసందేశవాక్యాలనుఅందించారు.
కావ్యారంభంలో, తిరుమలేశ! శ్రీనివాస!
నమోవేంకటేశ్వరా!
అన్నగర్భాక్షరభక్తినివేదనఉన్నది.
కావ్యంలోనిదశగీతాలలో

1) జననీజనకులదీవన
2) మనిషికదేఘనసాధన
3) మాతాపితరులుదేవతలు
4) ధాతరీతిగాజన్మదాతలు
5) వారలప్రేమసుధాజలధి
6) వారిసేవనవరత్ననిధి
7) వారిపలుకులేవేదములు
8) భక్తిపాత్రములుపాదములు
9) వారిదయకల్పభూరుహము
10) వారిపూజవరదాయకము

అన్నగీతసందేశాలుఉన్నాయి.
ఇందాకటిఉదాహరణలోవలెనేఒక్కొక్కగీతమాలికలో
నూమధ్యాక్షరాలనువరుసగాకూర్చుకొంటేఈపైవా
క్యాలువస్తాయన్నమాట.

చిత్రకావ్యాన్నిసమంజసభావగర్భితంగా,
ఉత్తమసందేశాత్మకంగారూపొందించాలన్నప్రయ
త్నంనిజంగామెచ్చదగినది.

గొప్పకళాకారులకు, విజ్ఞానవేత్తలకు,
మహనీయులకుఒకకళలోశిఖరాగ్రానికిప్రయాణించి
పరమావధినిచేరుకొన్నాక,
ఆకళలోఆశాస్త్రంలోపొందగలిగినవిజయాలేవీలేవ
న్నంతగావిజయాన్నిసాధించినతర్వాతతమకుసం
బంధంఅంతగాలేనివేఱొకరంగంలోగుర్తింపునుపొం
దాలనేతహతహపాటొకటిఉంటుంది.
ఆరెండవరంగంలోవారిప్రయత్నాలనుచూసిజనం
నవ్వుకోవటంకూడాఉంటుంది.
ఒకగొప్పచిత్రకారుడుఒకగొప్పకవినికూడాఅనిఅని
పించుకోవాలనిప్రయత్నించటం,
ఒకసంగీతవేత్తమఱొకశాస్త్రవేత్తగారాణింపునుకోర
టంమనముచూస్తూఉన్నదే. అయితే,
శ్రీనివాస్విషయంలోఅదిఅపవాదనిచెప్పవచ్చు.
ఆయనపెద్దగాకోరికలేమీకోరుకోలేదు.
తనకుఅభిమానపాత్రమైనసంగీతాన్నిఅభిమానంతో
అభ్యసించి, పొందగలిగినవిజయాలన్నీపొందారు.
తెలుగుదేశంలోకవిగానూ,
గాయకునిగానూగౌరవాదరాలనుపొందారు.
తనఅభివ్యక్తినిమెఱుగుపఱచుకొనేప్రయత్నమేత
ప్పఆయనఈకవితాకళమూలానభేరీభాంకారాలనుఆ
శింపలేదు.
ఆయనవ్యక్తిత్వంతోపరిచయంఉన్నవారందరికీతె
లిసినసంగతేఇది.

నిరంతరాయితమైనవ్యాసంగంతోరచనసాగించట
మేఆయనచేసినపని.
దానిలాభాలాభాలదృష్టిఉండేదికాదు.
ఐకాంతికమైనఅభ్యాసంకావటంవల్లఆయనరచనలో
సమకాలికకావ్యవిమర్శరీతులకుఅనురూపంగాసృజ
నశీలితనుతీర్చిదిద్దుకోవాలనేప్రయత్నంకనుపించ
దు.
తనకృతులనుఅధికరించిపఠితలఅభిప్రాయంఏవి
ధంగాఉంటున్నదీఆయనపట్టించుకోలేదు.
ఈలక్షణాలన్నీఆయనమలిరచనలైన'గాయకుడిగే
యాలు'అన్ననూటపదహారుగేయాలసంపుటిలోనూ,
Lovely Love Songs, White Shadows
అన్నఆంగ్లగీతికాసంపుటాలలోనూమనకుకనుపిస్తా
యి. ఇవన్నీఆయనవైయక్తికభావసంపుటులు.
ఆత్మీయాభివ్యక్తులు.
చిత్రకవిత్వకోవిదత్వంవల్లఆయనకుసిద్ధించినపం
క్తిపావనతకుఇవిఛాయారేఖలుమాత్రమేఅనినాఅభి
ప్రాయం.
సుకవిత్వానుభవికులకువీటిలోచర్వితచర్వణగాచి
త్తవిచ్ఛిత్తినికల్పింపగలఉదాహరణీయస్మరణీయ
పంక్తులు; భావికతకు,
భావుకతకునిదర్శనలుకనిపించవచ్చును.

'గాయకుడిగేయాలు'లోతనగురుతుల్యులుశ్రీసాలూ
రురాజేశ్వరరావునిసన్నుతిస్తున్నఒకగేయంకోహినూ
రు.
చాలామందికిపుస్తకంఅందుబాటులోఉండకపోవ
చ్చుననిఉదాహరిస్తున్నాను:

నిగనిగలకోహినూరు
నీముందుబలాదూరు!
నీమేనుపైడితేరు
నీవయసేపరువాలూరు!
బుగ్గచిదిమితేపాలూరు!
పూపెదవులలోతేనూరు!
కన్నులవెన్నెలవెలుగూరు!
కను
సన్నలవన్నెలసొగసూరు!
నవ్వురసాలరసాలూరు!
నడకలహంసలలయలూరు!
కంఠంమధురరవాలూరు!
కదిలేకేశాలిరులూరు!
ఒడలివిఱుపులోమరులూరు!
ఊహాలుమదిలోమెఱుపూరు!
తనువునిలువునావలపూరు!
–నా
మనసుసదానీతలపూరు

Notes:

1. From Mahakavi Kalidasa's "Kumara Sambhava"

2. Taken from an e-mail sent by M.S. Vasantalakshmi to the author.

3. Taken from Echchuri Murlidhara Rao's article.

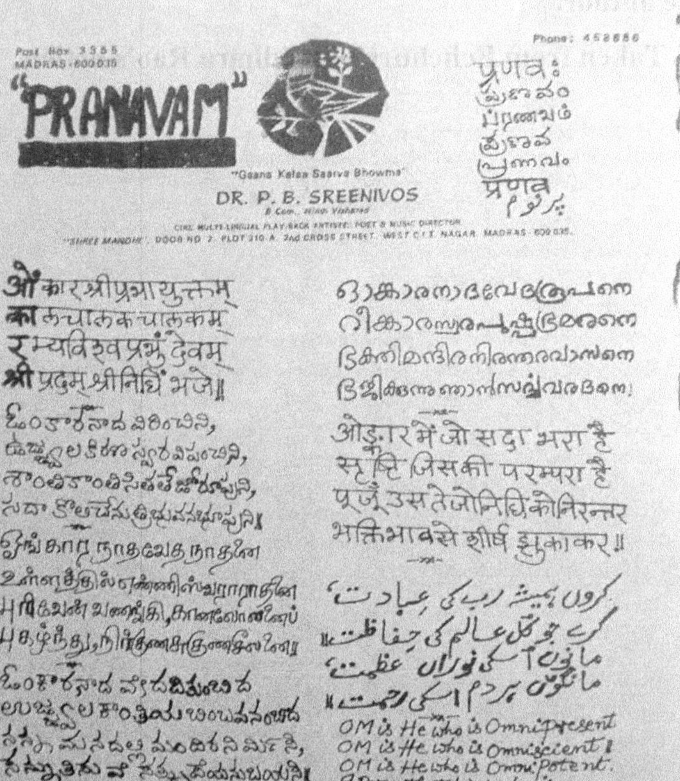

'ಪ್ರಣವಂ' ಕೃತಿಯ ಇಣುಕು ನೋಟ

Post Box 3555
MADRAS-600035

Phone: 452886

"PRANAVAM"

प्रणवः
ಪ್ರಣವಂ
பிரணவம்
ప్రణవ
പ്രണവം
प्रणव
پرنوم

"Gaana Kalaa Saarva Bhowma"

DR. P. B. SREENIVOS
B.Com., Hindi Visharad

CINE MULTI-LINGUAL PLAY-BACK ARTIST: POET & MUSIC DIRECTOR
"SHREE MANDIR", DOOR NO 2, PLOT 210-A, 2nd CROSS STREET, WEST C.I.T. NAGAR, MADRAS-600 035.

ओङ्कार में जो सदा भरा है
सृष्टि जिसकी परम्परा है
पूजूँ उस तेजोनिधि को निरन्तर
भक्तिभाव से शीर्ष झुकाकर॥

OM is He who is OmniPresent
OM is He who is Omniscient!
OM is He who is OmniPotent.
I Pray that Lord who is
OMNI PROFICIENT.

Cover page of PBS' book"Pranavam"

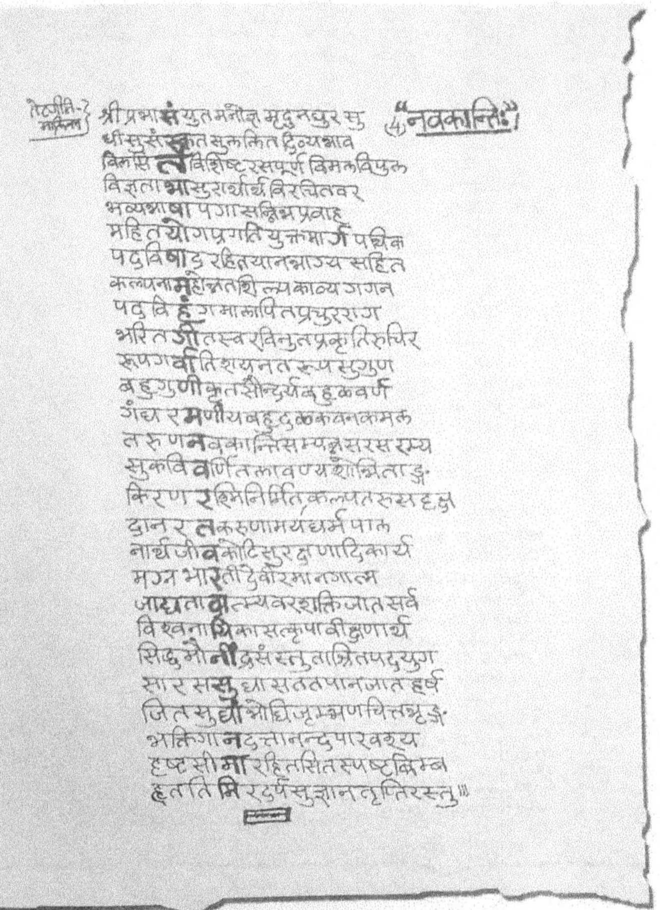

(4) "नवकान्तिः"

श्रीप्रभासंयुतमनोज्ञमृदुमधुरसु
धीसुसंस्कृतसुललितदिव्यभाव
विलसितविशिष्टरसपूर्णविमलविपुल
विज्ञताभासुरार्थार्धविरचितवर
भव्यभाषापगासन्निभप्रवाह
महितयोगप्रगतियुक्तमार्गपथिक
पदविषादरहितयानभाग्यसहित
कल्पनामहोन्नतशिल्पकाव्यगगन
पदविहंगमालापितप्रचुरराग
भरितगीतस्वरविनुतप्रकृतिरुचिर
रूपगर्वातिशयनतरूपसुगुण
बहुगुणीकृतसौन्दर्यबहुलवर्ण
गंधरमणीयबहुदलकवनकमल
तरुणनवकान्तिसम्पन्नसरसरम्य
सुकविवर्णितलावण्यशोभिताङ्ग
किरणरश्मिनिर्मितकल्पतरुसदृश
दानरतकरुणामयधर्मपाल
नार्थजीवकोटिसुरक्षणादिकार्य
मग्नभारतीदेवीरमानगात्म
जाग्रतावात्म्यवरशक्तिजातसर्व
विश्वनायिकासत्कृपावीक्षणार्थ
सिद्धमौनीन्द्रसंस्तुतार्चितपदयुग
सारससुधासततपानजातहर्ष
जितसुधाम्भोधिजृम्भणचित्तभृङ्ग
भक्तिगानदत्तानन्दपारवश्य
दृष्टसीमारहितसितस्पष्टबिम्ब
हृततिमिरदर्पसुज्ञानतृप्तिरस्तु ॥

A Poem in Sanskrit.

(4) "THE NEW LIGHT" . (4) "The New Light":

The traveller of life's journey, whose feat have the lack of fatiguelessness, and who has the great fortune of walking on the path of progress, entertains gentle divine thoughts, which flow like the river of an enchanting language, great by itself, endowed with the treasure of meaning, having been written with special radiant aesthetic sense, full of pure and vast vision of wisdom and improvised culture-oriented intellect, which shines with attractive, tender and sweet ideas, emerging from good knowledge! He revels in fine imagination, embellished with high sculptural beauty, as the birds of words, fly in sky of poetry, singing profuse modes and songs whose notes praise the effulgent beauty and bounty of Nature, whose pride bows before the beauty of virtues, which has more increased grace, like the Poetic-Lotus, which is multi-petalled, fragrant enriched by the youthful new light of celestial vision (appearance)! The inspired poet in the traveller, describes beautifully and juicily, the glowing form (body) of Nature, built by the scintillating rays which are benevolent and merciful like the Kalpa Vruksha, the boon-giving divine tree. The initial combined form and colossal energy of the three goddesses, Saraswathi, Lakshmi and Paarvathi, are always engaged in performing the duty of protecting the countless creatures, casting their very compassionate looks on the entire Universe, as they are the united leaders! For their mercy even the Saints and the Sages go on praising their feet, which give shelter to the woe-stricken souls. The blissful happiness of the Mind-Bee, which is obtained by drinking the nectar of their lotus-feet is definitely superior to the happiness of singing hymns of devotion. The traveller lost in such divine ecstasy gets the limitless clear vision of "Divine light of Spiritual Knowledge" which alone can dispel the arrogance of the darkness of ignorance. May that Divine Light bestow on him the not-easily attainable BOON OF CONTENTMENT !!

His Script in English.

13. "ఆత్మానందం"!

తుమ్మెద ఝుమ్మని పాడే గీతం!
కమ్మని స్వరాల మధుజలపాతం!!
తనువూ మనసూ మరిచే వేళ
తలపు తలపునా వలపుల లీల!!

కలల కొలనులో విరిసే కమలం,
అలల వలయాల కదిలే చెందం (అందం),
పులకలుగాని కని మురిసే భ్రమరం
సలిపే చిలిపితనం మకరందం!

ప్రకృతిలో సుమభ్రమర న్యాయం,
ప్రణయకావ్యాల స్వాధ్యాయం!!
ప్రకృతిపురుష సంయోగం యోగం!
ఫలప్రదం రసకేళి (పరవశ) భోగం!!

భ్రమర నాదమయ మాత్మానందం!
భావజీవమే పదసుమగంధం!!
అజరామరమీ అనుపమ గానం,
అనుభవమే పరమార్థ జ్ఞానం!!!
(పరమాత్మ)

A Poem in Telugu.

"వానవిల్లు"

భావాలను పుట్టినిల్లు తెలుగుభాష
పలువన్నెల వానవిల్లు తెలుగుభాష॥
అంతులేని సుధల జల్లు తెలుగుభాష।
అద్వితీయమనగ జెల్లు తెలుగుభాష॥

తెలుగులోపినే పాడును పాటల పులుగు!
తెలుగు మదికి హాయిగొలుపు వెన్నెల వెలుగు॥
తెలుపు కన్న నిర్మలమై వెలసెను తెలుగు।
తెలివికలిగి తెలుగు చదువ జ్ఞానము కలుగు॥

నవనీతమటన్న తెలుగు మృదు పదజాలం।
అవనీతల సురద్రుమం తెలుగు రసాలం॥
మంచి మనిషి మనసు కన్న తెలుగు విశాలం!
మార్పులెల్లగానుచే నిలుచు నిలకలకాలం॥

తెలుగువంటి మరొక భాష లేనేలేదు!
తెలుగుముందు తీయదనమె ఎంతో చేదు॥
తెలుగటన్న పట్టి మాట కానేకాదు।
తెలుగు విలువ వెలసెడ్కై నరానేరాదు॥

తెలుగు క్రొత్తదనము లూరి ఊటకెడు ఊట।
తెలుగు సుంతయైన చెక్కు చెదరని కోట॥
తెలుగు పరిమళాలు విరియు కవితల తోట।
తెలుగును స్వరనీరాజనమగు నీ పాట॥

తేలపూల కుసుమాల వర్ణహారము తెలుగు!
వలపురుచుల మఱపించే క్షీరము తెలుగు॥
పలుకులచెలి పలుకు పలుకు సారము తెలుగు।
నలువ సృష్టి మహిమ తెలుపు కేరము తెలుగు॥

కల్పనకే అందరాని తీరము తెలుగు।
కవిత మోయలేని అర్థభారము తెలుగు॥
నిర్గుణ గుణ వర్ణన కాధారము తెలుగు।
నిఖిలలోక భాషల పరివారము తెలుగు॥

In praise of Telugu.

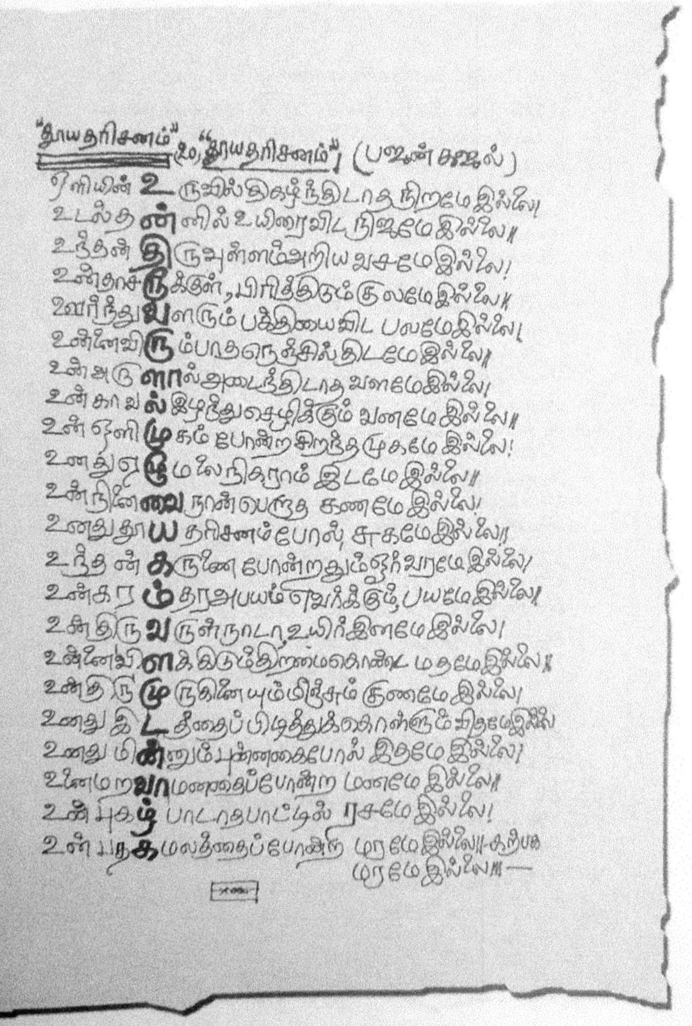

A poem in Tamil

(20, "The Sacred Appearance") (Thooya Darisanam)

Oliyin Uruvil Thigazhndidatha Niramē illai!
Udal thannil Uyirāi vida Nijamē illai!!
Unthan thiru Ullam ariya Vasamē illai!
Un daasarukkul, Pirithidum Kulamē illai!!
Oorinthu valarum bakthiyai vida balamē illai!
Unnai virumbaada Nenjil Didamē illai!!
Un arulaal adaindidaatha Valamē illai!
Un kaaval izhandu Sezhikkum vanamē illai!!
Un Olimugam ponra Sirantha Mugamē illai!
Unathu yezhu malai nigarām idamē illai!!
Un ninaivai Naan peraatha Kanamē illai!
Unathu Thooya Darisenam pol, Sugame illai!!
Unthan Karunai ponrathum oru Varamē illai!
Un karam thara abayam, yevarkkum Bayamē illai!!
Un thiruvarul Naadaa Uyir inamē illai!
Unnai vilakkidum thiramai konda Mathamē illai!!
Un thiru muruginaiyum Minjum Gunamē illai!
Unathu idathai pidithukkollum Vi[illegible]amē illai!!
Unathu minnum punnagai pol ithamē illai!
Unai Maravaa Manathai pponra Manamē illai!!
Un pugazh Paadaatha paattil Rasamē illai!
Un pada kamalathai pponra Maramē illai!–
Karpaga Maramē illai!!!

This composition is a specimen of acrostic style of poetry. Each fifth letter in each of the lines of the Tamil poem, reads the sentence (downward), "Un Thiruvarulaal Muzhu Vaiyagam Valamudan Vaazhga!" meaning, May the entire Universe progress and Prosper by your divine grace and mercy!!!

Tamil poem in transliteration

17. "The Happiness of Tamil Music"

Tamil language is Sweeter than nectar!
The aesthetic look at beauty goes the Tamil way!!
The eye of Tamil is a vessel of affection!
The Tamil-music gives Peace!!

—

The happiness given by Tamil Music removes Sorrow!
The Full Moon i.e Tamil emits Sacred light!!
The damsel of Tamil poetry is the Beauty-Queen of thought!
The path of Tamil prosperity is offered by Arts!!

—

The courteous Culture of Tamil is World-renowned!
The affection of a Tamilian is a peerless treasure!!
Tamil gives the clear vision, which conquers defeat!
Dear friend! Believe me! GOD'S grace is Tamil!!

—

There is a Special individuality in Tamil language!
Tamil flourishes gathering novelties, daily!!
The boquet of Art flowers Spreads Tamil-fragrance!
Madhuvandu performs service to Tamil!!!

—

Tamil-Damsel is the Gold-Peacock of Beauty!
She is the Cuckoo of flowery Sweetness and She is the Ganges of Music!!
She is the treasure-house of thought, whose name is Poetry!
The Seed of the Tamil vocabulary is the Divine Boon-giving tree!!

—

Poet Barathi, who enhanced the glory of Tamil is the charioteer of Public-Weal!!
Poet Kannadaasan's every Song tells the greatness and excellence of Tamil!!

—

When the music rendered by the voice of Maduvandu flows like a river, Tamil spreads light!!
Tamil Song wins any heart!
Tamil-mind always proceeds on the path of Progress!!

In praise of Tamil in English Language

In praise of Kannada language

(33) "കലാവാടിക"

കേരള നാടൊരു കലാവാടിക!
കേരള ഹൃദയം കൃഷ്ണനായിക!!
അനശ്വരതയാണ് രാഗമാലിക!
കേരള സംസ്കൃതി ദിവ്യഗായിക!!

ആസ്വാദിക്കാൻ സ്വരമകരന്ദം
ഭ്രമരമായ ഈ കേരളദേശം
നേടുന്നെന്നും പരമാനന്ദം!!
പാടാനുണ്ടൊരു മധുരാവേശം!!

കേരള ശ്രീനിധി പ്രകൃതി സൌന്ദര്യം!
നിരുപമമായതു് സുജനൗദാര്യം!!
സ്നേഹമാണ് കേരള ഐശ്വര്യം!
കേരളത്തിൻ വിജയ ശിരോധാര്യം!!

കേരള നാടെന്നും വാഴുക!
കേരള ഭാഗ്യം എന്നും വളരുക!!
രസികന്മാർക്കെൻ വിനയവന്ദനം!
നിത്യസമർപ്പണം ഹൃദയസ്പന്ദനം!!

സംസ്കൃതസംയുത മണിപ്രവാളം
കല്പനാനദി സുധാപ്രവാഹം!!
മലയാള കവിത നവനിധിയാണ്!
കലാസാധനകൾ നിരവധിയാണ്!!

കഥകളി നൃത്തം ബഹുപ്രസിദ്ധം!
മത്സരത്തിന് കേരളം സിദ്ധം!!
കേരളത്തിൻ കൃഷി [illegible]മാണ്!
കേരള [illegible]മാണ്!!

മലയാളികളുടെ നല്ല സ്വഭാവം
[illegible] ഉണ്ടു് [illegible] ഭാവം!!
മലയാളികളുടെ [illegible]
നേടുന്ന തൊഴിലുകളിലഭിവൃദ്ധി!!!

In praise of Kerala in Malayalam

(33) "The Garden of Arts"!

Kerala is the flower-garden of Arts!
Kerala's heart is replete with the love & devotion of Radha-Krishna!!
Its aesthetic sense is the garland of Modes!
Kerala's culture is itself a divine Songstress!!

Kerala has become a Bee, to taste the honey of Music!
Always emotionally inspired to sing, Kerala attains eternal bliss!!

The Beauty of bountiful Nature is the Wealth-Treasure of Kerala!
The prosperity of Kerala is sweet friendship!!
The call of Kerala has to be obeyed, bending the head in reverence!!

May Kerala live long eternally!
May the prosperity of Kerala be ever-growing!!
My humble obeisance to my Kerala-fans!
I dedicate always my heart-beats to them!!

[illegible]

Malayalam, replete with Sanskrit is Mani Pravalam.
It is the torrential flow of the nectar-river of imagination
Malayalam is the Treasury of Poetry!
Kerala's artistic achievements are in multitudes!!
Kerala's Katha-Kali Dance is World-renowned! Kerala is ever-ready for any competition!! Kerala's industry is endless! Kerala's success is Untransgressable!!
Malayalees' good nature is devoid of enmity!
Their sharp intellect is ever sure of industrial Prosperity

[illegible]

In praise of Kerala and Malyalam in English Language

(57) "A WONDERFUL MEDIUM"!

English is a veteran, versatile and impressive Universal Language!
English is very liberal and magnanimous, adding new words, in every Page!
English never gets old, as it is energetic and eternally young in age!
Achieving many glories, English enjoys multi-faceted advantage!

English should never be treated as a language alien & foreign!
English rules the literary world, with a mighty Power, Sovereign!
Even the hearts of the worst critics & antagonists, English Can easily win!
In almost all the other languages, English words find their kith and Kin!

English goes on developing tremendously growing to Colossal dimensions!
English offers full Scope for time-to-time innovations and inventions!
English is very capable of transgressing all types of interventions!
English can express very Precisely and lucidly, our thoughts, ideas & intentions!

Everyone accepts and hails the all-pervading capacity of English Poetry!
English can be described as a prolific Sweet-fruit-bearing Mango-tree!
English, of course, is opposed by many who entertain Prejudice & Bigotry!
All the same English can gain into any heart, by virtue of its virtues, Safe Entry!

English has seven letters, representing the Seven notes of Divine Music!
English can excercise on any Stubborn mind, its enchanting Magic!
On Inter-National Level, English has attained free flow of traffic!
Its impact on and influence on every walk of life are indeed terrific!

Amongst all the idioms of languages, English has its own Unique Idiom!
Amongst the most powerful media of culture & literature, English is a WONDERFUL-Medium!
English too does have certain lapses & handicaps, but they are minimum!
English Knowledge surely helps in countless ways, offering benefits, MAXIMUM!

People should not try to oust English, on selfish and prestigeous grounds!
Travelling around the World, English has completed already several rounds!
English, is no doubt, born to earn, by means of its innate values, eternal victory!
English has already made and will continue to make unprecedented HISTORY!

In praise of English Language

(59, "Silent Ocean"!

Let us not leave hope, though it leaves us!
Our hope is one which relieves us,
Nicely, from all the dark and sad thoughts;
Generously untieing our trouble-knots!!
Luck too bargains with loss and gain;
In time, bad luck turns good again!!
Views may be changing, from time to time,
Every change has its own rhythm and rhyme!!
Mind is the Sacred Temple of Peace!
Rising and falling emotions do cause worries!!
Having good control over each emotion,
Unchanging Man is a SILENT OCEAN!!
God plays, testing man's Patience,
He keeps man in turbulent emotions!
Life means Countless surprises;
Bringing many Sunsets and Sunrises!!
Unkind Time won't be ever unkind!
Rising sun sets but rises to find,
Lovely changes in the atmosphere,
Ending despair and its fear!!
So man should nourish Hope always!
Optimism is a PRISM of colourful rays!
Noble and bold minds receive GOD's benign grace!!!

A poem in English

CHAPTER 10

INIMITABLE HUMANIST

I

Songs of Enduring Impact

To many avid listeners of film music, P.B. Srinivos' singing invokes an image of a very decent and noble person.He was an embodiment of a cultured, refined and suave gentleman. His bass voice combines the sweetness of 'Baasundi' (the sweet he was particularly fond of), and the gentle breeze of the river Godavari.That's why a PBS song never jolts, but seeps into your psyche slowly, thus awakening a pain that lasts a lifetime, but is enormously pleasing to the ear.Every voice carries an 'aural character that defines its intrinsic quality'[1]. PBS' voice can easily be defined as 'soothingly gentle'. If you soak in any of his melodies sung in either of the eight languages, what you reap is ineffable peace and grace. Like his countenance and demeanour, his voice also sounds graceful, knowledgeable and profound. It is this unending grace in his voice that makes you succumb to its persuasive charisma even if you are not an ardent admirer of his singing skills.If the job of a great artist is to enhance the joy of human beings, it is evident that P.B. Srinivos was true to his muse, or rather his two muses- Sahitya and Sangeeta. Whatever could be said through music, he unfolded them through his 'gamakas'. He might not have a bundle of vocal inflections within the musical metre-as some of the classically trained playback singers like Ghantasala, P.Leela and P.Susheela had, yet the communication of mood, tone and pitch is so appropriately in sync with the overall sentiments of the songs that the listeners have no choice but to swoon to his charms.

The pristine gentlemanliness is clearly visible in some of the finest duets of Kannada, Tamil, Telugu and Malayalam film fields that he rendered with P.Leela, P.Susheela and S.Janaki: 'Pon en ben'("PoliceKaaran Magan"), 'Poovuvale virabuyavale'("Constable Kooturu"), 'Andala O Chiluka' ("Letha Manasulu"), 'Kannum en kannumay'("Minnunnatellamponnella"), 'Naane veene neene tanthi avane vainika'("Maavana Magalu"), 'Parthen sirithen'("Veerabhimanyu"). In the same manner, PBS sang appealing songs with Ghantasala, A.M. Raja and K.J. Yesudas:

'Madi Sharada Devi Mandirame' ("Jayabheri"), 'Paavana Bhaarata' ("Seetha"), and 'Aadiparaashakti' ("Ponnapuram Kotta")

Every co-singer of PBS had great regard for him. The tributes paid by the film fraternity indicate their assessment and admiration for PBS.

II

Philosophical and Ethical Approach

"A. **What is poison?**

Anything which is more than its necessity is poison: It may be power, wealth, hunger, ego, greed, laziness, love, ambition, or hatred.

B. What is Fear?

Non-acceptance of uncertainty is fear: if you accept uncertainty, it becomes adventure.

C.What is Envy?

Non-acceptance of good in others is envy: if we accept good, it becomes inspiration.

D.What is Anger?

Non-acceptance of things which are beyond our control is anger: if we accept it becomes tolerance.

E. What is Hatred?

Non-acceptance of person as he is: if we accept the person unconditionally, it becomes love."

-Rumi, a famous Turkish poet[2]

PBS, being a polyglot and bibliophile, read Arabic, Persian and Turkish poetry too. It appears that PBS followed the aforementioned words of a famous Turkish poet, Rumi to the 't'.

Like many cine artistes, PBS too experienced ups and downs in his life. He had competitors, detractors, back stabbers and rivals in the Southern Indian film field-even though he was 'Ajatashatru' who fought with none. For his downfall in Kannada and Tamil fields, a few artistes of the movie world - who ironically praise him today to the skies-were responsible. In contrast, he never harmed even insects. Even when he was fractured, he tried to save a cockroach; likewise, he saved a small bird who was caught in his car bonnet[3].

It is a well-known fact that PBS was a thorough gentleman: his genial nature, with the innate aversion for campaigning for himself or for using marketing techniques or projecting himself even in the days of cut-throat competition with the youngsters, was also responsible for the fading of PBS as a singer.He accepted uncertainty and accepted persons as they are and started loving the persons who harmed him. In this manner his approach was highly philosophical and ethical.

III

Comments and Tributes[3]

J.J.Jayalalitha:

Dr. P.B. Srinivos is indeed a multi-faceted genius, poet, musician and singer par excellence. Generations of Indians have basked in the mellifluous magic of his voice enthralled by the lilting dulcet of his melodious songs which have captured every mood, every emotion that man or woman can feel. “Pranavam” a collection of poems in eight languages is yet another marvel from the versatile and fertile mind and pen of Dr. P.B. Srinivos. In “Pranavam” we see the nobility of bhakti, beauty, faith, devotion, love, pathos, nature and nationalism flow gently and harmoniously along eight different streams.

Vishwanatha Satyanarayana (a famous poet):

After listening to the song ‘Ningi Lona Neeti Lona’, the famous Gyan Peeth award winner and writer of “Veyi Phadagalu” said, “PBS’s perfect male voice as it came from his naval (naabhi).”

Diwakarla Venkatavadhani (a famous Telugu scholar):

Even though PBS’ “Srinivasa Gayathri Vruttam” is a small book, it contains volumes of information about new ‘chandassu’ in Telugu.

M.S. Viswanath:

“PBS’ forte was his complete understanding of ‘Swaras’ and he could sing immediately listen to the score and the lyrics. He was very dignified in his conduct; his deep voice and unique tone easily blended into his songs…PBS was always quick to grasp what a music director, and above all he was blessed with a wonderful and mellifluous voice.”

Ghantasala:

PBS sang 'Oho Gulabi bala' song very delicately and impressively.Only he should sing such songs.Tammudu (PBS) sang 'Nilave ennidam Nerungathe' in Tamil very well. Why should producers insist on me to sing its Telugu version? it is their madness."

S.S. Vasan (Producer of Gemini Studios):

P. B. Srinivos' small humming is enough to melt the stones.

G.V. Iyer (Famous Producer and Director):

I have read the Vedas and the Puranas, PBS' 'Atma Vimochanam' can can melt even a stone-heart.

M.S. Subbulakshmi:

PBS is a special person. His achievement in light music is remarkable; his command over languages is enviable; and his simplicity is emulatable.

Talat Mehmood:

I have known PBS since the days of recordings in Gemini Studios. His pronunciation and accent of Urdu is perfect.

Lata Mangeshkar:

PBS' pronunciation of Urdu was far superior to that of many Hindi singers.

Asha Bhonsle:

PBS' voice is the most attractive romantic voice I have come across in the world of music. He is a genius. The felicity with which he renders 'gamakas' is really enthralling.

P. Susheela:

PBS was a great singer. He was a kind-hearted gentleman to the core. He used to persuade me to learn Urdu language and sing in Hindi.

S. Janaki:

PBS and I sang thousands of songs together. He was an excellent singer and writer; he wrote a number of songs in Hindi, Sanskrit, Telugu, Tamil and Malayalam for the movies and I sang some of them. He had a good sense of humour. He was a very good human being and a good teacher.

Jikki:

PBS'book titled "Pranavam" is a unique contribution to the world of literature. He is specially blessed by God to become a worthy Poet-Singer.

Vani Jayaram:

I grew up admiring and enjoying PBS' songs from my school days.They are all evergreen and immortal melodyPBS' mild nature. His voice was as refreshing as tender breeze.I was blessed to sing a few songs with him in Kannada.I sang a Tamil duet also with him. PBS' mild nature with quick sense of humor, humility and respect for fellow human beings should be emulated by the young singers. He was a rare human being to come across indeed.

K. J. Yesudas:

I have profound regard for PBS.He was friendly and well mannered. He always encouraged youngsters like me. We sang some songs together in Malayalam.

S. P. Balasubrahmanyam:

Shri PBS was 'AjataShatru' He had no enemies. He was a polyglot who wrote thousands of poems in 8 languages.When I sang an Urdu ghazal written by PBS in the presence of the then Pakistani High commissioner and other Pakistanis, they highly appreciated it.He called me L.G. Balasubramanyam as I was lucky to sing for M.G.Ramachandran almost in the beginning days of my career.He made me and my sister sing for Doordarshan some of the songs written by him in Telugu,

Tamil, Kannada, Malayalam and Hindi.He used to attend the concerts of a number of musicians and generously shower encomiums on them.He was a very good human being full of magnanimity.

P. Bhanumati (Multi-faceted Actress):

PBS is like a brother to me. He is a melodious singer with a magnanimous heart.

Rajkumar (Renowned Kannada Actor):

I am 'Shareera' (body in Kannada) and PBS is my 'Shaareera.' (voice in Kannada)

B. Saroja Devi (Renowned actress) :

PBS was a melodious singer: I like his voice and I some times recall his famous songs pictured in movies in which I acted with MGR and Raj Kumar

Bharati Vishnuvardhan (Renowned actress):

PBS was a very good singer and writer; he was humane and affable; he was enemy to none and had good relations with everyone; quite often I listen to my favourite songs sung by him. He was a cultural icon with an inbuilt melody in his voice.

T.L. Kanta Rao (Renowned Telugu actor):

PBS, for a long time, contributed to the growth of my career. He is fond of writing and singing Ghazals. He used to discuss his writings which were of higher level.

K. Jaggaiah (Renowned Telugu actor):

I often wonder at PBS' versatility: He is a polyglot, a genius and a rare combination of music and poetry

Chittibabu (Renowned Veena Vidwan):

In rendering the Ghazals, PBS reached the pinnacle of sweetness. His*kalpana shakti* (power of imagination) crossed the boundaries of the Earth.

Veena Gayatri (Veena Vidwan):

Sri.P.B. Srinivas' versatility and his multifaceted personality are well established facts. An exemplary singer and a genius par excellence, his melodious voice could execute almost every intricate nuance most effortlessly. My music director father, late Sri.G. Aswathama's all time first and best choice of male playback singer was Sri.P.B. Srinivas. Many hit songs of my father's were sung by SriP.B.S. My father and Sri.PBS also shared a deep understanding and friendship. The fact that they had great regards for each other added a lovely colour to the many Telugu hits composed by my father and sung by Sri.P.B.S. I personally loved the soft gentleness of his voice. According to me the subtle quality of his voice reached out to the deep recesses of the listeners' souls and left a permanent imprint in their hearts. At the age of 8, I had the great fortune of performing Veena in his presence. His heart was as large as his musicianship as he not only blessed me, but continued over the years to keep in touch with my artistic growth through constant support and encouragement. To my knowledge he is one of the very few artistes who openly and heartily encouraged young artists by attending their concerts, praising them publicly. His expression came from his excellent poetry in many languages. His grasp of Urdu and Arabic amazed me! His particular obsession for ghazals was revealed in the innumerable meetings I had with him. He would make sure everyone enjoyed whichever ghazal he appreciates. There was a touching childlike quality in him which was proof of his humility, the primary quality of greatness! I owe it to Sri.PBS for bringing out the singer in me. I had the fortune of singing with him for a private album called 'Dasa Geetha Geetha Sandesham', a compilation of songs penned and set to music by him. He was a great human being. Neither his fame nor his extraordinary musicianship made him egoistic and complexed which is generally the case. On the contrary he was down to earth and reached out to people through his warmth. I always found his optimism, easy going attitude and zest for life an inspiration to uplift my spirits. Though he has physically left this world, he breathes through the gems of his songs he has left behind for millions of his admirers.

Devi Ramana Murthy (Ghazal singer and daughter of famous Veena Vidwan, Eemani Shankara Shastri):

P.B. Srinivos is a name that echoes even today in the lush and evergreen musical abode of Playback singers of Southern India.He was an embodiment of knowledge and a walking encyclopaedia.Being a blend of his passionate literary work and glorious musical sojourn, PBS became a unique legendary figure and a Genius of All Times. If playback singing were his metier, Ghazal was his forte. PBS was a great admirer of Shahanshah-e-Ghazal, Mehdi Hassanand was inspired and influenced by Mehdi Hassan's extraordinary style of Ghazal rendition. P.B. Srinivos is still alive in the hearts of millions of people across the world.His Music,Poetry and Personality are cherished by one and all. I am humbled and honored to share my experiences during my long association with my Mentor, PBS.

K.S. Vasantha Lakshmi ('A' grade All India Radio artiste and Ghazal singer)

I loved PBS' songs in all the languages which he sang with such emotion. His voice had a very elite quality lending a soothing lilt to everything he sang. I feel like saying something about Mr. Srinivas' linguistic abilities. The songs he wrote were in such lucid, chaste and beautiful Telugu. It was real poetry. As a person who studied English literature, I was extremely touched and impressed at the quality of language as well as the metric rhythm and the ease with which they fitted into the tunes. Although the compositions were not easy having been based on Carnatic ragas, any singer would feel at ease to lend their voice to them. That was the beauty of the lyrics which were like pearls that would roll out of the voice of a singer.

Shivaram (Actor and Film maker):

I was lucky to have been associated with him since 1960; he was humble and simple; he was not avaricious and had excellent sense of humour; there is no replacement for PBS; also, I was lucky as some of his songs were pictured on me.

VAK Ranga Rao (Critic of Film music):

What all I have learnt from PBS, I can't learn from any University.

Vairamuthu (Lyricist):

PBS' songs are like the feathers of a peacock massaging my heart.

Dr. N. Devanathan (Former adviser to Chief Minister, A.P.):

Just as "Pranavam" acquired importance in the Vedas, Dr. P.B. Srinivos acquired importance in the galaxy of-especially after writing "Pranavam". He deserves to be called "Aasukavi".

Dr. Satyanarayana (Former Professor of ENT, Madras Medical College):

PBS' work conforms to the high ideals and higher faith in the spirit that pervades.

Dr. G.V. Subramanyam (Former Professor of Telugu, University of Hyderabad):

The book "Pranavam" by P.B. Srinivos should become epitome of Ingenuity and Higher Intelligence.

Dr. S.S. Mani:

Posterity alone will understand and appreciate PBS' versatility and selfless service.

Rajan (of the famous music composer combination Rajan-Nagendra):

PBS will never die. His lilting voice will forever reverberate in our ears.

B.K. Sumitra (Playback singer):

I sang duets and devotional songs with PBS. His songs reverberate in our ears. My voice has become famous as I sang with him: it was my 'purva janma sukrutam.'

Chiranjeevi Singh (Retired IAS officer):

Kannada is not my mother tongue; I learnt Kannada for understanding PBS' songs. His voice is a combination of the majesty of K.L. Saigal, the melody of Talat Mahmood, and the variety of Mohd Rafi.

Dr. Rajesh:

PBS is a combination of the Sun's brightness and the Moon's pleasantness; he is one of the stars on the firmament of Kannada film field.

K.S.L. Swami (Director, Producer and Actor):

I admire the way PBS writes down the song, practices the ragas, and sings for recording; I like his concentration, control over the modulations and his behaviour.

Dwarakish (Director and Actor):

PBS had a golden voice. His was an unforgettable voice in Kannada Chitraranga. He had made a big imprint on the minds of Kannadigas. Everybody wanted and admired PBS. He was disciplined and used to be punctual at the rehearsals.

Hamsalekha (Lyricist and composer):

He made tough compositions look easy through his singing. His fertile voice with a slight hint of nasal suited all kinds of songs. His songs from the movie “Kanakadasa” are superb.

Dore Bhagavan (Producer and Director):

PBS is a boon to Kannada film industry. He is a combination of ‘Sajjanata, Sowjanya and Sneha’.

Yograj Bhat (Lyricist and Film maker):

PBS had a devotional voice with an intimate tinge, which made everyone feel that he was close to them.

V.Ramnarayan (Editor, Sruti magazine):

What was special about PBS’ voice? It was a silken voice, unaffected and untrammelled by artifice - an apparently trained voice, conversant with the nuances of Raga music. I don’t know if he ever trained to be a classical musician, but he seemed so, the thousands of songs he composed in a variety of ragas more than sufficient proof of his knowledge of classical music. He was also a linguist, so many languages did he compose and sing in. His commitment and volume of output were extraordinary. Here was a true karmayogi in full view (and unmindful) of an admiring, often intrigued public.

K.S Ashwath:

PBS is a disciplined artiste.

Bangalore Nagesh:

PBS is an excellent play back singer

Manjula Gururaj:

PBS encourages young artistes

IV

Accolades and Awards[4]

1. **Doctorate conferred by Arizona State University, USA**
2. Ganakala Sarvabhauma
3. Pumbhava Saraswati Gana Samrat
4. Sangita Nadamuni (Sri Kanchi Kama koti Peetham)
5. Sangeeta Ratna (Sri Kanchi Kamakoti Peetham)
6. Sangeeta Kalanidhi (Sri Raghavendra Swamy Matham, Mantralayam)
7. Asthana Vidwan (Sri Raghavendra Swamy Matham, Mantralayam)
8. Light Classical Song Chakravarti
9. Kalaimamani (Govt of Tamil Nadu)
10. Karnataka Rajyotsava award (Govt of Karnataka)
11. Ugadi Puraskar (Govt of Andhra Pradesh)
12. Ugadi Puraskar (Telugu Academy, Chennai)
13. Panmozhi Paavalar (Bharati Paasarai)
14. Pustaka Bhushana Shiromani
15. Shivaji Ganesan Award
16. MGR Award
17. Gana Gandhrava (Karnataka Fans' Association)
18. R. Nagendra Rao Award
19. Vamsi Award (Vamsi RamaRaju, Hyderabad)
20. Akruti Award (Sudhakar Rao, Hyderabad)

21. Kaminkara Award ((Trivendrum)

22. Aravindan Memorial Award(Cochin)

23. President of Tamil Nadu Eyal Isai Natakam Mandram

24. Bharat Kalakar Award (YGP Institute Award)

25. Mudra Award

26. Kuzhalisai Kurlone

27. Arivuraignar (Adviser, Music schools, Tamil Nadu)

Notes:

1. T.M. Krishna, "A Southern Music: The Karnatik Story", Harper Collins, 2013.

2. Rumi was a famous Turkish poet.

3. Taken from a book by Srinath in Kannada "Madhurya Sarvabhowma Dr. P.B. Srinivos - Nadayogiya Sunsadayaana" and from the emails and audio files sent to the author.

4. Ibid

5. Taken from the book P. Senthamilselvi's "Innisai Chakravarthi P.B. Srinivos"

APPENDIX I
THE DIAMOND KEY

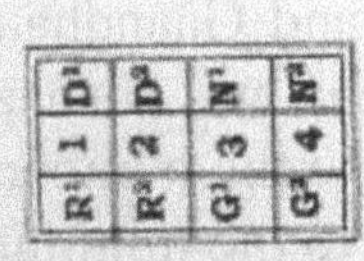

THE DIAMOND - KEY

TO THE 72 MELAKARTHAS

Conceived &
Designed by Dr. P.B. SREENIVOS

The 72 Melakartha Raagaas form the foundation for the creation of countless Janya Raagaas (Modes) and hence are called Janaka Raagaas. Earlier, P.B. Sreenivos, the noted cine playback artiste, studied deeply the structure of the 72 Melakarthas and evolved a simple mathematical principle, which served as a ready reckoner for finding out the actual notation of each Melakartha, when any chosen number is given out of the 72. The ready reckoner had been explained in detail a few months back over television, in Free India weekly, and also in a few colleges encouraging the study of classical music.

SIMPLE WAY

P.B.S., after further study, has invented a simpler approach to work out the notation of Melakarthas. He has conceived and designed a diagram in the shape of a Diamond-Key. which opens the treasure-house of the 72 Janaka Raagaas in lesser time - within a few seconds. Actually, the principle can be very easily followed by mental calculation, without any strain on the brain. Yet, P.B.S. has designed the Diamond-Key for the benefit of all musicians to provide a clear-cut idea about the method of approach.

Given a chosen number, divide it by six (6). If the number is more than 36, just deduct 36 from the given number and then divide by 6 as it is. When you get a balance (remainder), add 1 to the quotient. If the balance is zero (0), don't add 1 to the quotient, but treat zero as 6.

EASY METHOD

Now the quotient determines the Rishabha and Gaandhaara, whereas the balance determines the Dhaivatha and Nishaada of the chosen Raagaa. In this simpler principle the number of combinations to be remembered are reduced to the minimum, enabling a musician to get the results on the spot. Just six numbers are to be kept in mind. They provide also an easy method to be remembered.

12, 13, 14, 23, 24 and 34 are the six numbers employed by P.B.S. to unlock the Magic house of Melakarthas. Out of these six diamond numbers, as per the quotient and remainder (balance) only two numbers have to be selected, which represent the Ri Ga and Dha Ni respectively. In the numbers selected by P.B.S., there is a philosophical and moral significance too in the gradual course of calculation. The diagram of the Diamond Key can be drawn within a few seconds by memory and the notations can be arrived at on the spot, just by a specified mathematical calculation.

NEW VISTAS

P.B.S. believes that this simple method goes a longer way to help musicians of all calibres in the field of compositions, opening a new vista of countless permutations and combinations, for creating new Ragas and exploring the hitherto unexplored regions of Music.

His earlier invention of a new Chapter in PROSODY, the Science and Grammar of Poetry, (Srinivasa Gayathri Vitamins), has won blessings and appreciation of great savants. P.B.S. now hopes to gain the blessings and appreciation of the music maestros and students of music as well.

FIRST STEP

The earlier simple mathematical principle paved the way for this simpler method and this simple one may, in its turn, lead towards the simplest method, if any.

Search, research and invention end nowhere as they continue to realise possibilities of new depths and heights in the oceans and mountains of the vast Nature, i.e., God's creation.

P.B. Sreenivas feels that his latest contribution to Music and Poetry may be the first rung in the ladder of research towards the goal of Knowledge - the single and singular source as well as resource of eternal bliss.

DIAMOND-KEY CALCULATION

Out of the 72 Melakarthas, you may choose any number to find out the scale of that raagaa. Divide the number by 6. If the number is above 36, before dividing by 6, deduct 36 from the number.

For instance, take 48. By deducting 36 from 48 you get 12. Divide 12 by 6. You get 2 as quotient and zero (0) as remainder. When the remainder is 0 You have to treat it as 6.

As per the Diamond-Key, the six combinations of Rishabha 'R', Gandhara 'G', in poorvardh and Dhaivatha 'D' and Nishaada 'N', in uttaraardha are represented by 12, 13, 14, 23, 24, 34. Now, the quotient 2 denotes 13 and the remainder 6 denotes 34 in the above six diamond numbers. The Quotient always determines R & G, while the remainder determines D & N.

CONSTANTS

Now, in the 12 notes of music, S R1 R2 G1 G2 M1 M2 P D1 D2 N1 N2 S and P are constants. Whether the given Raagaa has M1 or M2 can be determined by its very number itself. If the number is 36 or less than 36, it has M1. If it is more than 36, the Raagaa belongs to the M2 group. Now for convenience

1, 2, 3, and 4 are selected to represent R1 R2 G1 G2 in poorvaardha (first-half) and DI D2 NI N2 in Uttaraardha (second-half) respectively. Hence, the Quotient 2 denoting 13 now proves that the Raagaa has R1 G2. Likewise, the remainder 6 denoting 34 proves that the Raagaa 48 has N1 N2.

Take another example. If you want to know the scale of Melakarta number 40, first deduct 36 from it. You get 4. Dj-vide 4 by 6. The quotient is 0 (zero) and remainder is 4. When ever you get a remainder other zero, you have to add 1 to the Quotient. Hence, you get the real quotient as 0+1. In this case, it is 1. Out of the six numbers of the Diamond-Key 12, 13, 14, 23, 24, and 34, in this case, the quotient 1 denotes 12 and the remainder 4 denotes 23.

In 12, 1 represents R1 and 2 represents R2. In 23, 2 represents D2, 3 represents N1 individually. Thus, you now have S R1 R2 M2 P D2 N.

Now take 26th Mela. This is M1 group because it is less than 36. So divide 26 by 6 directly without deducting 36 from it. Here you get 4 as the quotient and 2 as remainder. Because the remainder is not zero, add 1 to 4, the quotient. So the real quotient is 5 and remainder 2.

Out of the six Diamond-Key numbers 12 13 14 23 24 34, the 5th number 24 represents R2 G2 individually.

The remainder 2 denoting 13, determines D1, N1.

So the Scale of 26 Mela is S R2 G2 M1 P D1 N1.

APPENDIX II
SELECTED MALAYALAM HIT SONGS OF DR. P.B. SRINIVOS

Music Director :M.S. Baburaj

	SONG	MOVIE	LYRICIST
	Kanneerenthinu Vaanambaadi	Umma	P Bhaskaran
2.	Thallaanum Kollaanum	Umma	P Bhaskaran
3.	Allaavin Thiruvullam	Kandambecha Kotu	P Bhaskaran
4.	Ooruka Padavaal	Paalaattu Koman	Vayalar
5.	Bhaarathamedini Potti Valarthiya	Ninamaninja Kaalppaadukal	P Bhaskaran
6.	Maamalakalkkapurathu	Ninamaninja Kaal	P Bhaskaran
7.	Padinjaare Maanathulla	Ninamaninja Kaal	P Bhaskaran
8.	Thottillil Ninnu Thudakkam	Kuttikkuppaayam	P Bhaskaran
9.	Odippokum Kaatte	Porter Kunjaali	Abhayadev
10.	Pinneyumozhukunnu [Bit]	Porter Kunjaali	Abhayadev

11.	Poovaniyukilli niyum	Porter Kunjaali	Abhayadev
12.	Veedaayaal Vilakku	Chettathi	Vayalar
13.	Inakkuyile Inakkuyile (Thulasi Thulasi Vili kelkoo)	Kaattuhulasi	Vayalar
14.	Kocheekkaar athi	Thommante Makkal	Vayalar
15.	Nillu Nillu Naanakkuduk kakale	Thommante Makkal	Vayalar
16.	Sapthaswara sudhaa	Anaarkali	Vayalar
17.	Avalude Kannukal	Kaattumallika	Sreekumaran Thampi
18.	Rande Randunaalu	Kaattumallika	Sreekumaran Thampi
19.	Geethe Hridayasakhi	Poochakkanni	Vayalar
20.	Kaakkakondu kadal	Poochakkanni	Vayalar
21.	Evideyaanu Thudakkam	Baalyakaalasak hi	P Bhaskaran
22.	Karlin Kannuneer Mukil	Baalyakaalasak hi	P Bhaskaran
23.	Nin Rakthamente	Baalyakaalasak hi	P Bhaskaran
24.	Asthamanakk adalinnakale	Sandhya	Vayalar
25.	Kaaviyudupp umay	Sandhya	Vayalar

Music Director V. Dakshina Murthy

S.No.	SONG	MOVIE	LYRICST
1.	7Aniyaay Puzhayil	Amma	P Bhaskaran
2.	Innum Kaanum	Naadodikal	P Bhaskaran
3.	Kaanmu Njan	Seetha	Abhayadev
4.	Lankayil Vaana	Seetha	Abhayadev
5.	Paavana Bharatha	Seetha	Abhayadev
6.	Prajakalundo Prajakalundo	Seetha	Abhayadev
7.	Seethe Lokamaathe	Seetha	Abhayadev
8.	Kezhaathe Kanmani	Jnaana Sundari	Abhayadev
9.	Chandanakkinnam	Vidhi Thanna Vilakku	P Bhaskaran
10.	Karakku Kampani	Vidhi Thanna Vilakku	P Bhaskaran
11.	Munnottu Poku Sahaja	Viyarppinte Vila	Abhayadev
12.	Thedithediyal anju njan	Viyarppinte Vila	Abhayadev
13.	Mannavanaay aalum	Sathyabhaama	Abhayadev
14.	Thaskaranalla Njan (Bharathastre ekalthan)	Susheela	Vallathol
15.	Kannilppettathu	Devaalayam	Abhayadev

16.	Karivala Karivala	Inapraavukal	Vayalar
17.	Swapnangal Swapnangal	Kaavyamela	Vayalar
18.	Ee Muhabathenth oru	Kannoor Deluxe	Sreekumaran Thampi
19.	Kannundaaya thu Ninne	Kannoor Deluxe	Sreekumaran Thampi
20.	Nabhramir Nathoyam	Jagadguru Adisankaran	Sankaracharya r
21.	Paryankatha m Vrajathiya (Guruvandana m)	Jagadguru Adisankaran	Sankaracharya r

Music Director: G. Devarajan

S.N o.	SONG	MOVIE	LYRICIST
1.	Abhoomi Kuzhichu	Kalanjukittiya Thankam	Vayalar
2.	Niranja Kannukalode	School Master	Vayalar
3.	Vana Devathamaar e	Shakunthala	Vayalar
4.	Michelangelo [Charithrathint e Veedhiyil]	Jail	Vayalar
5.	Ormakale	Arakkillam	Vayalar
6.	Dhoomarash mithan	Kasavuthattam	Vayalar
7.	Vanee Varavanee	Sheelaavathi	P Bhaskaran
8.	Onnam Kandathill	Velutha Kathreena	Sreekumaran Thampi

9.	Padmaasanat hil	Kumaarasambha vam	Vayalar
10.	Kavithayo Ninte kannil [Kathaprasang am]	Aa Chithrashalabha m Parannotte	K Sivadas
11.	Kezhakku Kezhakkoraan a	Thriveni	Vayalar
12.	Ammayum Nee	Navavadhu	Vayalar
13.	Priyathama Priyathama	Navavadhu	Vayalar
14.	Oru Matham Oru Jathi	Achanum Baappayum	Vayalar
15.	Zindabaad Zindabad	Maasappadi Maathupilla	Yusufali Kecheri
16.	Aadiparaasha kthi	Ponnaapuram Kotta	Vayalar
17.	Muthu Mehboobe	Prethangalude Thaazhvara	Sreekumaran Thampi
18.	Sree Bhagavathi	Devi Kanyaakumaari	Vayalar
19.	Amme Maalikappurat hamme	Durga	Vayalar

Music Director: Lakshmanan

S.No.	SONG	MOVIE	LYRICIST
1.	Kaimuthal Vediyaathe	CID	T.M.Nair
2.	Nillu Nillu	CID	T.M.Nair
3.	Mahal Thyaagame	Harishchandra	T.M.Nair

4.	Avaniyil Thaano Njan Akappeduvaa no	Aana Valarthiya Vaanampaadi	T.M.Nair
5.	Jodiyulla Kaale	Aana Valarthiya Vaanampaadi	T.M.Nair
6.	Om Kali	Aana Valarthiya Vaanampaadi	T.M.Nair
7.	Enthininiyum	Christmas Raathri	P Bhaskaran
8.	Ninne Piriyukil	Sreeraama Pattaabhishekam	T.M.Nair
9.	Pokunnitha	Sreeraama Pattaabhishekam	T.M.Nair
10.	Thaathan Nee Mathavu	Sreeraama Pattaabhishekam	T.M.Nair
11.	Thannepol Thante (Kalvariyil)	Snaapaka Yohannan	T.M.Nair
12.	Azhakil Mikachatheth u	Atom Bomb	T.M.Nair
13.	Romeo Romeo	Atom Bomb	T.M.Nair
14.	Jeevitham Oru Kochu	Priyathama	Sreekumaran Thampi

Music Director: K.Raghavan

S.No.	SONG	MOVIE	LYRICIST
1.	Vaanile Manideepam	Neelisaali	P Bhaskaran
2.	Kanninaal	Krishnakuchela	P Bhaskaran
3.	Pattiniyaaluyir Vaadi	Krishnakuchela	P Bhaskaran

4.	Jayabheri	Unniyaarcha	P Bhaskaran
5.	Om Shuklaambar adharam (Slokam)	Unniyaarcha	
6.	Prathikaara Durge	Unniyaarcha	P Bhaskaran
7.	Udavaale Padavaale	Unniyaarcha	P Bhaskaran
8.	Baliyallaa	Rebecca	Vayalar
9.	Iniyoru Jananamundo	Rebecca	Vayalar
10.	Muzhangee Muzhangee	Rebecca	Vayalar
11.	Nithyasahaay a Naadha Bit	Rebecca	Vayalar
12.	Maanasam Kallukondu	Ramanan	Changampuzh a
13.	Sthree Hridayam	Kodungallooram ma	Vayalar
1 4.	Sreemahaaga nesha Sthothram (Pancharathn a)	Utharayanam	

Music Director: Ghantasala

S.No.	SONG	MOVIE	LYRICIST
1.	Devi Radhe	Shaanthi Nivas [D]	Abhayadev
2.	Sree Raghuram	Shaanthi Nivas [D]	Abhayadev

Profiles of PBS in different headgears.

ABOUT THE AUTHOR

Dr. Ranganath Nandyal has worked on the faculty of English for 30 years in some prominent Universities in India and abroad. He received Ph.D. from Andhra University in 1983 and was a Postdoctoral Fellow at University of California, Los Angeles during 1985-86. He has contributed research papers to prestigious journals and newspapers. His book on Henry Miller received rave reviews in India and abroad. Having retired as Professor of English, he is presently doing research in the field of musicology.

His book on the Legend Ghantasala has received good reviews from scholars and film personalities like Gyan Peeth Award winner Prof. C. Narayan Reddy and Dada Bhai Phalke Award winner K. Vishwanath.